Integrative Psychotherapeutic Approaches to Autism Spectrum Conditions

of related interest

Counselling People on the Autism Spectrum
A Practical Manual
Katherine Paxton and Irene A. Estay
ISBN 978 1 84310 552 7
eISBN 978 1 84642 627 8

Asperger Syndrome and Psychotherapy
Understanding Asperger Perspectives
Paula Jacobsen
ISBN 978 1 84310 743 9
eISBN 978 1 84642 613 1

Mental Health Aspects of Autism and Asperger Syndrome
Mohammad Ghaziuddin
ISBN 978 1 84310 727 9 (paperback)
ISBN 978 1 84310 733 0 (hardback)
eISBN 978 1 84642 105 1

How Everyone on the Autism Spectrum, Young and Old, can...
become Resilient, be more Optimistic, enjoy Humor, be Kind, and increase
Self-Efficacy – A Positive Psychology Approach
June Groden, Ayelet Kantor, Cooper R. Woodard and Lewis P. Lipsitt
Foreword by V. Mark Durand
ISBN 978 1 84905 853 7
eISBN 978 0 85700 520 5

Aspies on Mental Health
Speaking for Ourselves
Edited by Luke Beardon and Dean Worton
Part of the Adults Speak Out about Asperger Syndrome series
ISBN 978 1 84905 152 1
eISBN 978 0 85700 287 7

Integrative Psychotherapeutic Approaches to Autism Spectrum Conditions

Working with Hearts of Glass

 David Moat

Jessica Kingsley *Publishers*
London and Philadelphia

First published in 2013
by Jessica Kingsley Publishers
116 Pentonville Road
London N1 9JB, UK
and
400 Market Street, Suite 400
Philadelphia, PA 19106, USA

www.jkp.com

Library of Congress Cataloging-in-Publication Data
Moat, David.
   Integrative psychotherapeutic approaches to autism spectrum conditions :
working with hearts of glass / David Moat.
       pages cm
   Includes bibliographical references and index.
   ISBN 978-1-84905-388-4 (alk. paper)
   1. Autism spectrum disorders--Treatment. 2. Autism spectrum disorders in
children--Treatment. 3. Psychotherapy. I. Title. II. Title: Working with hearts of
glass.
   RC553.A88M656 2013
   616.85'882--dc23
                                        2013000394

British Library Cataloguing in Publication Data
A CIP catalogue record for this book is available from the British Library

ISBN 978 1 84905 388 4
eISBN 978 0 85700 750 6

Printed and bound in Great Britain

Contents

Acknowledgements

My first contact with the autism spectrum came some three decades ago, when I left the world of banking and insurance to work in a residential project for adults with autism. The world of residential care services – and, indeed, autism – is very different now, but I am indebted to those 18 adults, and their families, for enabling me to begin my journey alongside the spectrum. Further gratitude is due to all the people on the spectrum I have met since then, as I have continued that journey. I have been privy to some remarkable stories, and this has fed my understanding and rapport with autism, as well as teaching me so much about myself.

My career in psychotherapy has overlapped with my autism journey. I am grateful to Professor Jure Biechonski and his colleagues for their encouragement towards exploring the value of psychotherapeutic techniques for autism. Further thanks must go to all those in my ever-expanding world-wide network of fellow counsellors and therapists, who have so willingly, and valuably, shared experience and ideas with me.

There have been times whilst writing this book that I have virtually ignored my wife, Emma, and yet still she has supplied me with support, sustenance and, above all, love. It is in this depository that my especial thanks must be placed.

Introduction

Autism is characterised by elements of atypical functioning in the areas of communication, social interaction, and flexibility of thought, as well as potential difficulties in sensory integration. These circumstances mean that people on the spectrum will have ways of perceiving the world that are different to the norm. It is these areas of different functioning that can lead to problems in 'connecting' to one's human environment, and can thus create the potential for conflict and stress. Perhaps some of the behaviours displayed by people on the spectrum could be described as defensive, or reactive to these circumstances, in much the same way as more neurotypical people might react to stress or distress.

I have observed elsewhere that, for most people, the place of psychological and emotional strength is usually at the centre of a strong, supportive network, where we feel acknowledged, accepted and embraced.[1] The absence of acceptance and affirmation in our lives is likely to create emotional difficulties. I see a number of people across the whole range of autism who have poor self-awareness, poor self-esteem and a very fragile personality. These issues may present themselves as anger or anxiety-related dysfunction, or depression, and any of these can be the result of having to live in situations where one simply doesn't fit.

Thus it can be said that an autism spectrum condition in itself can cause emotional distress, and this can be exacerbated as the result of feeling disconnected, or misunderstood. This distress can be worked through using various psychotherapeutic approaches.

Key Principles

A major clue to opening up pathways of working lies in acknowledging the autism and its effects. Autism is characterised by functional differences in communication, social understanding, flexibility of thought and sensory integration. In therapeutic terms, these elements can be described as primary stressors. They can create a perception and perspective on the world that is very different to that of other people. If we add a learning disability to the profile, then those perspectives and perceptions will be altered yet further. These issues are bound to lead to high levels of social and emotional stress. Understanding these perspectives is vital to successful therapy.

A second clue to successful working is understanding that whilst a person's autism may be a major feature of that person's life, there are other things going on for that person as well, as they do for other people. We all react and respond to our environment; we all have individual personality traits; we all have a genetic inheritance of some sort; and we all have an experience of life. Each of these things affects who we are and how we react to things. In autism, the impact of these things may be distorted, but that does not mean we should discount them.

Third, a therapist should understand that autism affects those around the individual perhaps at least as much as it does the individual themselves. An awareness of projection (a psychological phenomenon in which a person attributes unwanted feelings to another person), and introjection (the internalisation of such projections), is vital in unravelling the sometimes complicated relationships that can develop around the individual. A similar awareness of transference and counter-transference is also necessary. Here, a client may 'transfer' feelings about a significant person onto the therapist. Counter-transference refers to the reverse process, where a therapist needs to be aware of their emotional reactions to the client. Understanding a little about group dynamics and disrupted functioning can also be useful. This can be especially helpful when considering the effects of the human environment around the spectrum client.

Other Factors

A solely medical view of autism risks ignoring emotional stress. A solely behavioural approach risks becoming stuck in 'symptom management'. A combination of the medico-behavioural perspectives risks over-reliance on pharmacological interventions. An integrative and holistic psychotherapeutic approach can help to avoid these risks and lead to very real and lasting progress.

Another factor which is involved in poor outcomes and overall prognosis is negativity. A doctor might say to a parent, 'I'm sorry, but your child has autism…' A mainstream school might view the autistic child as a nuisance. Peers might view the child as strange or odd. Poor social functioning might create isolation and loneliness. And thus the child may develop poor self-esteem, low confidence and a lack of motivation. These things can then lead to anger, frustration, depression and anxiety as the child grows up. Each of these emotional elements is treatable using psychotherapeutic approaches.

Autism affects those around the individual in various ways. This is sometimes overt, as in the case of a parent who quickly becomes depressed and/or frustrated. Sometimes the effect is more subtle, where these things happen over a longer period of time. But sensitive psychotherapeutic approaches can also benefit everybody within the autistic person's network.

And if the network functions well, it can only be good for the individual at the centre of it.

This book seeks to explore ways of helping to promote emotional wellbeing on the autism spectrum. The importance of rapport is introduced, followed by discussion of some of the key psychotherapeutic approaches that may be of use. Some of these are expanded in more detail through later chapters. We follow a path that moves from relaxation techniques, through social networks, into Cognitive Behavioural Therapy. We will look at working non-verbally with individuals, perhaps through using play and creative approaches. The journey takes us through the use of hypnotherapy and guided imagery, story-making, anger and anxiety management, before finally taking us into Positive Life Planning. The appendix discusses newer approaches, such as Emotional Freedom Technique and Eye Movement Desensitisation and Reprocessing, and will look at some of the historical perspectives around therapeutic approaches for autism.

Defining Terms

I understand autism to be more of an umbrella term covering a range of possibilities, rather than a useful diagnosis in itself. Despite decades of research, diagnosis is still very reliant on behavioural observation (and is thus quite subjective), and the term 'Autism Spectrum Disorder' (some prefer 'Autism Spectrum Conditions') has to cover an entire continuum. Currently, this continuum starts at 'classic' autism (which might be described as autism with a severe learning disability), moves through 'high-functioning' autism (autism with perhaps a mild or moderate learning disability), and ends for many at Asperger Syndrome (autism with no learning disability). It also has to cover a range of presentation within each of these categories. Examples include: verbal/non-verbal/partially verbal; poor eye contact/good eye contact; hyper-sensitivity/hypo-sensitivity; isolated and withdrawn/socially inappropriate. Thus, to say that someone has autism conveys very little information at all about an individual, beyond a potential sharing of some key characteristics, and practitioners have to guard against making assumptions upon which erroneous treatment is based. This can risk exacerbating the very problems that the practitioner is trying to help solve, assuming that the practitioner has not already decided to refuse therapy for the spectrum client on the grounds that the client cannot enter into the social contract due to his or her disability. Later on, we shall see examples of how we can engage in therapy for even severely learning disabled people with autism.

I understand psychotherapy to be another umbrella term, covering a range of therapeutic options designed to enable people to develop better psychological and emotional wellbeing. It may involve traditional 'talking' therapies, but can also involve more creative techniques such as play, music, art, dance, movement, etc., as well as hypnotherapy. Therapists who combine a number of these disciplines are often referred to as Integrative Psychotherapists, and I count myself among their number.

The description 'neurotypical' is often used to characterise people who do not share an autistic perspective on the world. It was first coined within the community of people with an autism spectrum condition.

Some practitioners may be surprised to note the absence of a specific chapter on depression in this book. It is woven into the text at several points in various chapters, but I have avoided the temptation to devote a whole chapter to it, on the grounds that I believe depression to be a reactive defence used in response to experiences and circumstances. It is not, in itself, an emotion – it is more a symptom of an emotional system being thrown out of balance. There are sometimes clear indications for the use of anti-depressant medication for certain patients, or for the use of cognitive behavioural strategies. But, as Bill Goodyear (2008, p.66) points out, resources are sometimes used towards the short-term goal of managing depression at the expense of investment in a longer-term goal of creating confidence, happiness and self-esteem.[2]

Whilst there are a growing number of people with autism spectrum conditions undertaking training in counselling and other therapeutic interventions, it is currently more likely that a spectrum client will be seen by a neurotypical practitioner. However, the value of this book is not intended to be limited to this last group. It is hoped that practitioners of any neurological orientation will be able to use the information here presented.

Disclaimer

Many of the techniques discussed in this book are in the remit of trained professionals, who will have received adequate instruction not only in how to deliver the approaches safely and ethically, but also in how to manage difficult situations when they occur. This book is not designed to be a training or instruction manual, and should not replace robust, professional and accredited training in aspects of psychotherapy, hypnotherapy, Neuro-Linguistic Programming, play therapy, or any of the other approaches mentioned. The book is a guide for autism-aware practitioners to the various techniques that might form part of an integrative psychotherapeutic approach. For information about specific training, readers are directed to the various therapeutic professional bodies and associations.

Neither is it recommended that any of the techniques discussed should be applied in any specific case without appropriate consultation with the client and interested parties. Practitioners should also be aware of the provisions of legislation around child protection and the protection of vulnerable adults.

People with autism are individuals, which means that no two people on the spectrum are alike. Hence caution should be exercised with approaches that have been successful with other people – they may not work with the next client. Additionally, people with autism spectrum conditions have the right to be fully consulted on matters of treatment and intervention.

Despite these notes of caution, the following pages contain a wealth of information about the various techniques that constitute an integrative approach to the autism spectrum. Practitioners are invited to explore, and to enjoy, building an integrative therapeutic relationship with spectrum clients.

Chapter 1

Acknowledged, Accepted and Embraced

The place of psychological and emotional strength is usually at the centre of a supportive and positive network, where one feels acknowledged, accepted and embraced. Or, as Leo Kanner, one of autism's first pioneers, put it in 1969, 'Every child, every adult, everybody wants what I call the three "A"s: affection, acceptance and approval. If the child has that, regardless of his IQ or anything else, he will be all right.'[3] Many clients on the autism spectrum who are referred for counselling or psychotherapy often talk about feelings of disconnection within their environments. For example, Neil Shepherd (2011, p.104), a man with Asperger Syndrome, observed that 'Aspergics, like all autistics and any disabled people, have to deal with a world that isn't designed for them.'[4] This can drive the emotional responses that lead to anxiety, depression, anger and withdrawal. Thus the first rules of psychotherapy in general can be applied as the first rules of psychotherapy for autism – the creation of a safe environment in which to explore emotional responses, and the development of rapport and trust in the therapist/client relationship.

Rapport, and listening, are the starting points for a therapeutic relationship. It is sometimes difficult for a neurotypical therapist to understand and appreciate the subtleties and nuances of an autistic presentation. This can lead to an experience of further rejection, and affects the motivation to engage with further professionals. A client with Asperger Syndrome once asked me, 'How do I know you're not just another professional in a very long line of professionals whose sole purpose in my life has been to fuck it up?' Negative experiences tend to lead to a negative presentation, and it is beholden upon the therapist, when meeting a new client on the autism spectrum, to find ways of ensuring early positivity. I tend to use the 'five-minute rule' – I strive to make the first five minutes of the session positive, thus providing five minutes of positive experience on which to build the next five minutes. This seeks to avoid repeating the cycle of negativity experienced by many of our spectrum clients, which often started in early childhood with the oft-repeated message, 'There's something wrong with Johnny,' or the apologetic delivery of the diagnostic conclusion – 'I'm sorry, your child has autism.' Of course, many people's autism journey is much more positive, but I am talking here of clients who are referred for therapeutic support in various degrees of distress. Negativity often produces low self-esteem and low levels of confidence and motivation. This in turn produces feelings of frustration, depression, anger and anxiety.

So how can the neurotypical therapist establish the all-important rapport with a spectrum client? The first step to building rapport has been noted within the Neuro-Linguistic Programming (NLP) community as the art of establishing harmony, recognition and mutual acceptance between people who are at ease with each other (Chapters 2, 5 and 10 contain more information on NLP and its application to various issues). The therapist does this by noting the communication style, perspectives and body language of the client. These can then be reflected back to the client to help him or her feel more comfortable. This is a very empathic approach. It requires the practitioner to remember that the person with autism is probably running a completely different perception system to that of neurotypicals. It is ironic that people with autism are often described as demonstrating poor empathy towards other people, and yet neurotypicals can sometimes be accused of having the same problem when trying to understand the inner world of the person with autism.

Part of the different functioning is seen in the area of social interaction. For example, social anxiety can be so acute that a potential spectrum client feels unable to attend initial appointments. Or a client may feel so 'safe' within the therapeutic space that he or she begins to behave inappropriately. Perhaps the client avoids eye contact (or engages too strongly).

Sensory integration problems might also present difficulties to the therapeutic relationship. For example, a client may attend for an initial appointment, but quickly leaves the waiting area if a small child is crying, vowing never to return. In a therapy centre where practitioners share rooms, the smell of a previous aromatherapy session can linger, and prove to be overwhelming to the next spectrum client. A ticking clock or other background noise may distract. There might be a request for lights to be turned down if the spectrum client feels it is too bright.

There may be communication issues. A therapist might be faced with a non-verbal client (or one who is selectively mute). Traditional talking therapy will not be appropriate here. Verbal clients may obsessively talk about their favourite subject or interpret everything the therapist says literally. They could have difficulty describing their feelings (they could even have difficulty recognising their emotional state). Daniel Goleman (1996) attributes the first use of the term *alexithymia* to describe this situation to Dr Peter Sifneos in 1972.[5]

The autistic inflexibility of thought may mean that therapy sessions become fixed parts of a client's routine. Thus fixed-term therapy contracts might create anxiety as the final appointment approaches. Unforeseen cancellations and the like can also cause anxiety.

Hence it can be seen that the spectrum client can be confronted with a range of potential difficulties during an initial appointment (or even before). The autism-aware therapist will seek to ensure that these difficulties do not prove to be insurmountable. I tend to issue a referral form in advance of a first appointment. This form requests information about communication, social interaction, flexibility of thought, sensory integration and medical history. With this information I can prepare for the initial consultation – perhaps we will need an alternative waiting area, and I might have to ensure that our session does not follow someone else's aromatherapy treatment. Additionally, I might have to rearrange furniture to avoid an intimidating 'face-to-face' session, perhaps having both chairs angled slightly so that they are both pointing at a spot on the opposite wall. Prospective clients might ask for on-line counselling, which takes away many of the potential pitfalls. And maybe I will take account of other things that are highlighted on a client's referral form, such as needing to use concrete language, or being prepared for the first session to be dominated by a favourite subject in order to allow the client to use his or her favourite anxiety-management strategy.

Once the initial session is under way, the therapist can begin to observe the language (if any) used by the client, as well as body language, etc. It will be particularly useful to try to assess the preferred processing style of the individual. Is the client a visual thinker, therefore having a preference for visual processing? Or perhaps there is a preference for auditory, digital (reading/writing) or kinaesthetic thinking. A skilled practitioner may be able to pick these things up through conversation. Alternatively, the therapist can carry out a more formal assessment using one of the various VARK (Visual/Auditory/Read-Write/Kinaesthetic) assessment tools, many of which are available on-line.[6] Temple Grandin (1996) has written that visual processing is likely to be a default learning style for many on the autism spectrum.[7] Wendy Lawson, in her foreword to Olga Bogdashina's book on *Sensory Perceptual Issues in Autism and Asperger Syndrome* (2003),[8] reminds us that many people on the spectrum have different cognitive styles, and in particular refers to monotropism, or single channelling – there is little room for multi-channelling, or multi-tasking. Further reminders of the different styles and perspectives employed by people with autism are provided by Donna Williams (1998) in her book about autism and sensing.[9] A recent client of mine warned me on the first session that there would be long silences between being asked a question and her answer. She explained that she would need to 'translate' what I'd said into a visual image. She would then need to alter the image to provide a pictorial answer, before 'translating' that picture into the words that she felt I needed. Oliver West (2007) has usefully written about strategies for visual thinkers, in his ground-breaking book *In Search of Words*.[10] Another client would launch into a few minutes of 'waffle' about computers after any question, comment or observation that I offered, before finally, and seamlessly, placing his perfectly considered answer into this verbal stream. He described it as putting up a screen while he processed the question and came up with the answer – he did not like awkward silences!

What this means is that a counsellor or therapist (or teacher, carer, coach, mentor, etc.) needs to be able to 'think outside of the box' when approaching work with a person on the autism spectrum. In other words, they need to 'think inside the autism box'. The referral form will be useful in framing the initial session, but the therapist will also need to be skilled in the art of listening to behaviour, and body language, as well as the words used by the client. In short, the practitioner may need to do a little work in order to be able to create that all-important safe space. The practitioner will also need to factor in potential processing times into any fixed-term therapy contracts.

Normality Within Autism

Having focused on the essential differences between 'autistic' and neurotypical processing, it is worth noting that a good rapport between counsellor and client will enable areas of normality to be recognised. Whether a client has autism or not, there will often be a sense of relief if a therapist can reassure the individual that at least some of his or her experiences are typical of the general population. For example, any child might become withdrawn and isolated if bullied at school – the withdrawal is simply reactive to a set of negative circumstances. It is easy to 'blame' everything people with autism or Asperger Syndrome do on their condition, and this risks a failure to help the individual deal appropriately with their past experiences. I once asked a spectrum client what she thought of the concept that all of us have a little autism in us. She replied, 'It means that there might be a lot of "normal" in me!'

Chapter 2

Integrative Psychotherapeutic Principles

We do not inhabit a 'one size fits all' world, and this is nowhere more true than in the fields of counselling and psychotherapy, and the field of autism. Thus having a range of tools in a therapeutic toolkit can be very useful. It enables a therapist to see a range of clients, and to offer a range of interventions. This is not to denigrate those counsellors and therapists who choose to specialise within one approach. It is certainly true that such people can develop a lot of skills and expertise within their chosen discipline, whilst some integrative practitioners can be accused of being a 'jack of all trades, master of none'. However, responsible and professional counsellors will ensure through supervision and continuing professional development that they are proficient and up-to-date in all the disciplines in which they operate.

The value of psychotherapy for autism can be seen from looking at a number of examples of distress that seem prevalent on and around the autism spectrum. We can consider:

- stress

- anxiety

- depression

- anger

- family distress/disrupted functioning

- post-traumatic stress reactions

- behavioural difficulties

- obsessive and compulsive tendencies.

This is not an exhaustive list, but highlights just some of the areas where individuals can have difficulty. All of these are susceptible to psychotherapeutic intervention in the neurotypical population and there is no reason to ignore such potential treatment within the 'autism' population. As has been mentioned above, it will be important to ensure that an understanding of the effects of autism is held by the practitioner. Perhaps of paramount importance will be an understanding of the particular effects of the individual's personal experience of autism. This is where information gathering and the development of rapport become essential to enable the therapist to start in the right place. In my experience, the best place to start is where the client actually is, rather than where we might want him or her to be.

Another advantage of a therapist and client sharing an understanding of the history and current situation of a case is the opportunity for looking at things from different perspectives. Some spectrum clients that I have seen are prone to describing life as a series of sometimes unconnected negative events (a similar situation is sometimes seen in depressed clients from the general population). Rumination on these events often drives negative thinking and expectations, thereby reducing motivation. I have often mapped out (literally), or charted, a client's history with a view to gaining an overall perspective first of all, followed by an exercise in filling in some of the gaps between the negative events with positive information. 'Reframing' activities of this type are often carried out verbally in 'normal' talking therapies, the idea being that we can sometimes change the perception of a situation, or picture, by putting it in a different frame. Providing an external visual reference can be very useful for clients on the autism spectrum, who, as we have seen above, may have a default visual processing system.

Once rapport and useful perspectives have been established, it will be possible to identify potentially useful strategies for therapeutic intervention and lifestyle suggestions. Additionally, it will be possible to acknowledge (indeed, for some clients, to 'name') the presenting issues. Some clients are referred because it is clear that they are depressed, angry or are experiencing social anxiety. The whole point of the referral is because treatment is being sought for these specific issues. Others may have difficulty in acknowledging or recognising their shifting emotional states. They may attend with a non-specific, or general, anxiety disorder. The referral may be to do with 'behavioural' difficulties. Or there may be an overall lack of motivation. For these clients, assessment, observation and interaction by the therapist can help in identifying and 'naming' the key problems.

Potentially useful psychotherapeutic strategies are discussed in detail over the remainder of this book. It will suffice here to introduce some of the key approaches to demonstrate the value of being able to combine disciplines where appropriate.

Cognitive Behavioural Therapy (CBT)

Our cognition (the way we think) can have a direct impact on the way we react (or behave). Changing our thinking can result in a change in behaviour. CBT is often hailed as the treatment of choice for autism spectrum conditions, particularly for people with Asperger Syndrome. Gaus (2007),[11] Jacobsen (2003)[12] and Paxton and Estay (2007)[13] all write eloquently on the subject. For the general population, CBT is also seen as a high priority for psychological treatment. In the UK, thousands of new cognitive behavioural workers are being trained in response to government initiatives to channel many National Health Service patients towards CBT under the auspices of the Improving Access to Psychological Therapies (IAPT) scheme. This is based on recommendations by the National Institute for Health and Clinical Excellence (NICE) which is keen to ensure that suitable patients (often having depression and anxiety-related disorders) are treated using empirically supported psychological treatments. Such thinking has been informed by research projects such as that undertaken by Richards and Borglin (2011) into the efficacy of CBT-type approaches.[14] A criticism of this type of research is that it is not comparative – it simply measures outcome rates of CBT alone. (At least one other research project conducted by Falk Leichsenring in 2001 showed no significant difference in treatment outcomes for depression between CBT and short-term psychodynamic psychotherapy.[15])

There is little doubt that CBT fits the cognitive profile of many people with high-functioning autism or Asperger Syndrome. However, both Attwood (1998, p.158)[16] and Paxton and Estay (2007)[17] highlight the need for the therapist to modify the approach to reflect the presence of an autism spectrum condition. They recommend the use of more visual strategies, for example, as well as reiterating the need for the use of concrete concepts in some cases.

Whilst CBT most definitely has its uses, some clients who have been to see me have had negative experiences with it, and specifically request alternative approaches. Some have experienced catastrophic and ruminative thinking, and found that a pure CBT approach simply made them better at thinking negatively. Others have found it difficult to establish a good therapeutic relationship with a pure CBT practitioner, particularly one without an appreciation of the autism spectrum. One client described his experience as leaving him feeling valued only as a statistic: 'My CBT person was not interested in me as a person – he seemed only interested in filling in outcome forms…' In these circumstances, an important part of building a therapeutic relationship will involve respecting these experiences, and being able to offer sensible alternatives.

Neuro-Linguistic Programming (NLP)

Neuro-Linguistic Programming can be said to be closely related to CBT, in that it focuses on the way that our thinking or perspectives influence our self-talk (and indeed our outward talk), which in turn can influence our expectations and behaviour. It enables the presentation of different perspectives, and can lead to greater behavioural flexibility. It utilises visual imagery, and thus its application in the field of the autism spectrum can easily be seen. There is an essential focus on the building of rapport, an important psychotherapeutic principle. Bill Goodyear (2008)[18] recognised the usefulness of NLP in the field of coaching people with high-functioning autism and Asperger Syndrome, and built a successful practice around it. If it is true that people with an autism spectrum condition have difficulty navigating a social world that is not designed for them, then any approach that helps to establish various different perspectives and that offers pointers to more effective performance is going to be helpful. Such approaches will be even more effective if the client is not reduced in the process to the status of mere compliance.

Hypnotherapy

Further visual and imaginative work can be achieved with the use of hypnotherapeutic interventions. Hypnotic states, once induced, can enable a subject to deeply relax and, if necessary, focus on particular thoughts and feelings at a different level of consciousness than the usual, everyday awareness. Hypnosis can also help with other issues, such as social anxiety, phobias, pain management, etc. It is a valuable tool in an integrative psychotherapeutic approach – it can combine neatly with both CBT and NLP, for example.

There are clear ethical issues around the use of hypnotherapy – it is an approach that needs explicit and informed consent. It is very difficult for people on the autism spectrum who have additional learning disabilities to provide such consent, but some spectrum clients with Asperger Syndrome have specifically asked for hypnotic intervention. This has been with a view to aiding relaxation, working through sleep difficulties, dealing with phobias and, in the case of some recent clients, the management of social anxiety. Conversely, some clients with Asperger Syndrome have requested not to receive hypnotic techniques, because their perception is that it involves a loss of control. A more detailed discussion of hypnotherapy and its application to autism spectrum conditions can be found in Chapter 8.

Relaxation

This is a key area for many people on the autism spectrum. Constant exposure to social stress and anxiety often means that a person with autism is hyper-vigilant and can experience physical tension. Sometimes the core cognitive processing difficulties mean that an individual has trouble sleeping. One client informed us that, 'My brain just won't switch off at night – I have to process all the things that have piled up there during the day.' An integrative therapist will often offer to teach relaxation techniques alongside any other therapeutic intervention that is being provided. Relaxation approaches can often be combined with hypnotherapy (indeed, relaxation is a key factor in hypnotic interventions, and can be a very useful way of helping a client to 'feel' what it is like to undergo hypnosis).

Meditation and Mindfulness

There is a growing understanding on the practical benefits of meditation for people on the autism spectrum. Chris Mitchell (2008), an author with Asperger Syndrome, has usefully contributed to the relevant literature.[19] Meditation can be a useful way of helping with relaxation (often because it provides a focus for thinking). Mindfulness has developed within modern psychological approaches over recent years – it utilises non-religious meditation, and again provides a deliberate focus (a purposeful paying of non-judgemental attention). It can provide excellent ways of viewing different perspectives, and can contribute to reframing someone's point of reference. Mindfulness can also help in improving social attention – people on the autism spectrum are often described as paying little heed to the needs of others, and the art of focused listening can be a useful tool in getting on better with folk.

Alternatives to Talking Therapies

In general, 'talk' therapies are aimed at people with sufficient intellectual capacity to engage with such approaches. This does not mean that psychotherapy cannot be offered to clients with autism and additional learning disabilities. Intensive Interaction is an example of a system designed to enable engagement at a non-verbal level. Key figures in the use of Intensive Interaction, such as Phoebe Caldwell (2007),[20] or Dave Hewett, Graham Firth, Mark Barber and Tandy Harrison (2011),[21] talk about using body language and mimicry to build emotional engagement and communication. Elements of Sensory Integration Therapy can also be used to assist in these cases. For example, sensory distress can lead to anxiety within particular environments, and working around some of the sensory issues experienced by some people on the autism spectrum can reduce difficult reactive behaviours. Additionally, creative and play approaches will be helpful in enabling better emotional and communicative expression.

I have also used some of these approaches with some clients with Asperger Syndrome, where, for example, verbal communication of emotional issues has proved difficult. For one or two such clients, 'talk' therapy can become an endless intellectual sparring with the therapist, without ever reaching a resolution. Using techniques that involve 'switching off' verbal interaction, we can begin to access underlying feelings.

Social Coaching

Anxiety can be a major factor in social confidence and performance across the autism spectrum. Isolation and withdrawal is often a defensive strategy employed in reaction to this anxiety. In working with some spectrum clients who have presented issues around depression, further investigation can reveal that they are lonely. I have noted elsewhere that appropriate coaching can often help to improve social performance and reduce these feelings of loneliness.[22]

Anger and Anxiety Management Approaches

There can be great benefit from the use of techniques to help individuals manage anger and anxiety. Anxiety can lie behind a number of reactive behaviours, including isolation and withdrawal. Anger can be the underlying emotion behind a range of difficult or negative behaviours. Concerns about either anxiety, anger or behavioural issues lie behind many of the 'third party' referrals to my clinic (where somebody else other than the client makes the initial contact).

Loss and Bereavement Work

We are beginning to explode some of the myths involving learning disability and autism spectrum conditions around bereavement. For many families and practitioners, grief was something to protect people with learning disabilities from. Hollins (2000) lists death and bereavement as one of the 'three secrets' kept from people with learning disabilities (the other two being sex and dependence).[23] Pat Howlin (2004, p.294) has observed how some people on the autism spectrum appear to show little, or an inappropriate, reaction to the death of a close family member, leading some to think that they do not care.[24] Noelle Blackman (2003, pp.49–58) observes that unacknowledged grief and bereavement issues can lie beneath changes in behavioural patterns, even if such grief is not expressed in the normal way.[25] Hence the value of 'autism-aware' counsellors being able to guide spectrum clients through their own individual bereavement pathway.

Positive Life Planning

People with autism are often described as being poor at planning. Techniques that support effective and positive planning can be at least as useful as strategies to deal with emotional problems. At a micro level they can help the individual to be better prepared for situations and to avoid potential hot spots. At a macro level, they can help to ensure appropriate and healthy lifestyle choices in terms of accommodation, employment, and social activities, etc. Elements of coaching and mentoring can be used as part of this type of support.

Imagery and Story-making

This approach combines elements from hypnotherapy, play, creativity and NLP. It can build towards a very effective way of enabling the safe exploration of difficult emotional material.

The fact that many people on the autism spectrum already have favourite characters and themes can be utilised. These can be used to provide ways of seeing different perspectives. Life story work can be another valuable way of exploring different perspectives, and can be useful in helping individuals to realise that they may be able to exercise some element of control over their lives. One advantage of this type of approach is that it can easily be adapted to suit the intellectual or developmental capacity of the individual.

…And Breathe!

People on the autism spectrum often experience hyper-vigilance, tension, disrupted sleep, intrusive thought patterns and a general inability to relax. Anxiety and panic attacks can also be present. Strategies to aid relaxation will therefore be of clear benefit. Such strategies easily fit alongside other therapeutic interventions and can introduce clients to the 'feel' of hypnosis, if necessary. A number of common relaxation systems are discussed below.

Breathing Techniques

Breathing techniques are useful where a person feels he or she might be about to experience a sudden peak of anxiety or a panic attack. Such techniques can be used in some cases of intrusive thoughts, and they are also very helpful for achieving general relaxation. Where a person is sceptical about such an approach, I have found that it is possible to gain a commitment to at least try one by using a simple logical explanation. For example, I might describe the physiological and chemical effects of using a breathing strategy. This can help a spectrum client understand the process, and enables better choices to be made about engaging with it.

A common breathing strategy is called 'diaphragmatic' or 'abdominal' breathing. This is often used in yoga or Pilates. It involves deep inhalations, ideally through the nose, expanding the abdomen rather than just the chest. Some practitioners advise counting when inhaling and exhaling in this way. I generally advise people to count to seven with each breath. Some clients can comfortably manage counting to a slightly higher number, whilst others prefer a smaller number. The process can be repeated between five and ten times, several times per day. In the unlikely event of a client becoming dizzy or faint, or if the process is painful, the exercise should be stopped immediately, and alternative relaxation strategies will need to be considered.

Deep breathing as described above can clearly increase the amount of oxygen available for absorption through the lungs, with potential physical benefits. More importantly for some is the psychological benefit of using this technique to maintain a mindful focus on breathing, rather than on the impending stress, anxiety or intrusive thoughts, etc. Where a client experiences sudden anxiety, such as during a panic attack, the process can be varied by replacing the outward slow breath with blowing the air out.

Progressive Relaxation

Edmund Jacobson (1938) is credited with first formulating the process of achieving relaxation by tensing and then relaxing specific muscle groups, one after another.[26] With this technique, a client will be taken through the process, and advised to repeat it regularly themselves. A typical sequence following Jacobson's suggestions might look like this:

1. right foot

2. right lower leg and foot

3. entire right leg

4. left foot

5. left lower leg and foot

6. entire left leg

7. right hand

8. right forearm and hand

9. entire right arm

10. left hand

11. left forearm and hand

12. entire left arm

13. abdomen

14. chest

15. neck and shoulders

16. face.

Variations on this sequence are possible. For example, some people might prefer to tense both feet at once, and so on. Others might prefer to start at the top and work down. The key issue is in experiencing the deliberate physical release of tension, together with the mindful focus on the various parts of the body. In time, it is possible to simply use the memory of the relaxed feeling to shortcut parts of the process. It is essential to advise clients to avoid getting up too quickly after practising this technique, thereby avoiding potential dizziness. A useful suggestion might be along the lines of, '…and when you've enjoyed this relaxation for a little while, simply count backwards slowly from five to one before stating "Now I can get up, feeling very calm, but fully alert".'

For clients who experience problems with remembering, or transferring learning from one environment to another, it is useful to provide a recording of the relaxation sequence for use at home (or whilst travelling perhaps, where there is social anxiety). Similar sequences can be used to assist falling asleep where necessary.

Craske and Barlow (2006)[27] observed that patients with Generalised Anxiety Disorder often experience an increase in anxiety or frustration when they first try to use such techniques. They noted that these feelings tend to diminish with continued practice of the technique.

Relaxation Techniques to Assist Sleep Problems

Some people on the autism spectrum experience emotional distress as a result of difficulties in going to sleep, or not being able to get back to sleep after waking in the night. For some, this is the result of the mind only really being able to process information received during the day when all other stimulation is significantly reduced – that is, when everyone else has gone to bed. A potential solution here is to provide more low-stimulation time during the day – perhaps additional down-time at school or work, for example. Another suggestion might be to avoid activities that are over-stimulating during the evening.

Further support can be found in the use of the progressive relaxation techniques mentioned above, with a specific focus on getting to sleep. Some people have found that the use of a recording specifically aimed at either getting to sleep, or at getting back to sleep, is useful. A sample script is given below for those wishing to create their own recording. It should be recorded using a calm, and soothing, voice. The script can be altered to suit individual circumstances.

If you're listening to this recording, it probably means that you have woken up, and are looking for help in getting back off to sleep again…and as you lie there awake, and think about being awake, all you can think of is not being able to go back to sleep…and as you think about not going back to sleep, your mind takes you to all kinds of places…and you just can't get back to sleep.

But there is no need to worry…your mind is a wonderful thing, and it will do just as you tell it to do…but first you need to make sure that you are relaxed…and your mind can help you to do this…and the first thing to do is to direct your thoughts inwards…and as you direct your thoughts inwards you may become aware of the rise and fall of your chest as you breathe…and you know that breathing is a natural process, and each inward breath draws in fresh, clean air, and provides your body with the oxygen it needs…and each outward breath helps to get rid of toxins and carbon dioxide…and all this happens automatically, helping the body to function in a balanced way…and as you focus on your breathing you may be able to see how it slows down…and you could take a deep breath in…hold it…and then a deep breath out…and in… and out…and enjoy that feeling of relaxation that is brought about…so that even if sleep is some way off, at least you're relaxing…

…and as you breathe, and relax, you may be able to notice the feel of the air against your face, and the feeling of the bed clothes on your body…and you can move your mind inwards again…inwards so that you can be aware of your whole body, or just a part of it…and you may be able to move your consciousness up and down your body from the top of your head to the tips of your toes…feel how heavy your head is on the pillow…and how heavy your body is on the bed…you can slowly wiggle your toes and when they are still they are relaxed…and you can slowly lift your knees up and lower them…and feel how they relax…and then clench your fists, and release them…press your elbows into the mattress, and then let them relax…and perhaps push your head back into the pillow, and then allow your neck muscles to relax…

all the while feeling how your entire body is becoming more relaxed…

…and it may be that you need to repeat this process again, or it may be just enough…and if you feel relaxed enough perhaps this will enable sleep…and if sleep is still some way off, at least your body is relaxed…and perhaps you might begin to drift off to sleep by counting slowly in your mind from one to ten, picturing each number written in front of you, but fading before you reach the next number…

In the case of some children with autism spectrum conditions it is sometimes useful to identify a favourite character and then to use references to that character within the script. For example, a story could be told about Thomas the Tank Engine relaxing after a long day at work, eventually becoming so relaxed that he falls asleep.

Music and Sound

Calm, peaceful music is an obvious aid to relaxation, and its use is widely recommended. However, the atypical processing styles of spectrum clients might require a degree of investigation, assessment, or trial and error to identify the particular music (or indeed sound) that can best achieve relaxation. A past client of a colleague found that he could only relax significantly whilst listening to heavy metal music played loudly through headphones. He explained that, 'It is the only thing that shuts out all the background noise that disturbs me so much.' There are various collections of music and sound effects available on CD, or as MP3 files available for download, and indeed a growing number of relevant applications for smart phones and portable computing devices.

Sensory Relaxers

It has been noted that children on the autism spectrum, in particular, may have an atypical sensory integration profile.[28] Such children will naturally be drawn to particular textures, or the 'feel' of things running through their fingers (sand, pebbles, water, for example). They may have a default self-stimulation activity (often called 'stimming'), such as twiddling a piece of string in front of their eyes. Observation of some of these activities can provide clues as to things that can be offered if a child becomes over-stimulated or anxious. Such assessment might identify a need for tactile toys and objects to assist relaxation, or perhaps a need to provide particular scents at critical times.

Temple Grandin (1992) has described in detail the potential benefits of deep touch pressure for people with autism.[29] Her belief is that, for some people on the spectrum, deep pressure is more calming than a light touch. She describes her own experiences of using a self-designed 'squeeze machine'. Lise Pyles (2002, p.193) makes further suggestions for enhancing deep pressure experiences for children with Asperger Syndrome.[30] She recommends weighted blankets and weighted jackets, for example. Wendy Lawson (2012) has commented on her use of a SQUEASE™ vest (an inflatable pressure vest that can be worn under other clothing, which can be activated inconspicuously at times of stress).[31]

Massage, aromatherapy and reflexology are additional ways of achieving relaxation. Clearly, some people on the autism spectrum will have difficulty tolerating certain kinds of touch or aroma, and practitioners need to be respectful of such preferences. Some clients can be introduced to massage (and be taught to tolerate more generalised touch) through the use of reflexology first. A past spectrum client at our clinic stated that his feet were far enough away from the centre of his being for them to be safely touched. After a few weeks he was able to tolerate chair massage and this proved a major enhancement to his ability to relax.

The use of multi-sensory rooms can also contribute to relaxation and enhance a sense of wellbeing. Such environments make use of a range of equipment to achieve this, including bubble tubes, projectors, fibre optic lighting, mattresses, ball pools, aromatic scent dispensers and sound systems.

Thought Stoppers

Negative and repetitive thought patterns can often spiral out of control, and for some people can trigger anxiety, anger and depression. Such situations are often reported by spectrum clients attending my clinic. This kind of ruminative thinking can remove focus from the task in hand, and thus interfere with academic performance or productivity at work. I have often suggested to clients that if they can catch the thought pattern early enough, then they can employ a 'thought-stopping' technique. This will enable a refocus back to the required task, or, if appropriate, it will help towards relaxation/sleep.

Successful thought-stopping tactics will vary from person to person. Some spectrum clients have the imaginative capacity to deliberately generate positive thoughts or affirmations. However, others will lack this ability, and may benefit from 'scripting' – the provision of ready-made words and statements that can be used to counter the negative thinking. Combining these approaches with a deep breathing technique can be helpful. It may also be possible to add a 'STOP' visualisation to the process. Here, a client would be advised to create a mental image of the word 'STOP', either all at once, or one letter at a time. Each of these approaches deliberately directs the conscious thought process away from the negative thoughts.

James and Gilliland (2011) describe a further technique for stopping negative thought patterns using an elastic or rubber band placed around the wrist.[32] The band can simply be pulled out from the wrist and let go – the result is that it snaps back against the wrist (not recommended for clients who are hyper-sensitive to small levels of pain). The instant slight irritation that this causes can interrupt a flow of thought, allowing scope for redirection, or for relaxation.

Exercise

Jordan and Jones (1999, p.61) restate the often-quoted fact that physical exercise can lower anxiety levels and heighten the sense of wellbeing,[33] thus enhancing relaxation. Some people on the autism spectrum can find it hard to engage with exercise, especially if their early experiences of it are intimidating and anxiety provoking. A logical explanation of the benefits can be helpful, as well as an exploration of possible environments in which to carry out particular activities. Sensory issues will play a part here, too. For example, a busy gym may have too great a sensory impact for some. Conversely, an agoraphobic reaction to open spaces can mean that outdoor exercise is problematic.

Trampolining is a popular example of how exercise can promote relaxation and wellbeing. Rebound Therapy® is described by Eddy Anderson (2012), its founder, as a way of promoting balance, communication and relaxation, as well as exercise.[34] It is repetitive (and therefore autism-friendly) and provides cardiovascular stimulation. Perhaps more importantly, in terms of relaxation, it allows sensory integration feedback. This creates the circumstances for the body to reach an equilibrium leading to a feeling of relaxation.

Chemical Relaxants

Chemical relaxants include prescription medicines, natural or homeopathic remedies, alcohol, nicotine and substances such as cannabis. Discussion of these here does not imply any endorsement or judgement. They are mentioned simply because they are amongst the range of additional support for relaxation used by people on the autism spectrum, in some cases with extremely positive results. There are clear contra-indications, side-effects and dangers which can be ascribed to a number of these relaxation methods, and none should be considered without appropriate medical advice.

Temple Grandin (2011, p.225) has spoken about the positive use of medication such as propranolol (a beta-blocker) and very low doses of Prozac to manage anxiety in autism.[35] Propranolol is often prescribed to people with high blood pressure, and thus caution should be exercised where a patient already has low blood pressure. Grandin also notes that people on the autism spectrum can react atypically to anti-depressants such as Prozac. For example, too high a dose can lead to agitation and excitability – exactly the opposite effect one is looking for when trying to relax!

Many people take a view on the efficacy of natural or homeopathic remedies in the treatment of a wide range of disorders and conditions. Examples of these approaches include the use of chamomile, lavender scent and various 'rescue' remedies. Controversy has arisen around whether the treatments are any better than placebos. However, such remedies are less likely to have as many side-effects as other, more conventional medications. Some preparations are readily available in health stores. The field is potentially difficult to navigate because of the somewhat entrenched rhetoric exhibited by proponents and opponents of natural remedies, and the absence of replicated large-scale research projects. Grandin (2011, p.171) suggests using the 'three families' or 'three individuals' rule to help to adopt a scientific approach to deciding whether to try a remedy or treatment.[36] This is a simple expedient, involving interviewing three families or individuals who have used the particular approach. Each family or individual is asked specific questions, such as, 'Was anything else introduced at the same time?' and 'What were the exact improvements that took place?'

The use of cigarette smoking and alcohol to manage stress and aid relaxation is widely noted amongst people on the autism spectrum and neurotypicals alike. Many people with social anxiety use low levels of alcohol to enable a more disinhibited engagement with what they might see as socially stressful environments. The health and addiction risks of both nicotine and alcohol are almost universally acknowledged, and a sole reliance on either (or indeed any chemical relaxant) to aid relaxation is probably an indicator that the individual might need support of a therapeutic nature to better manage, or avoid, anxiety.

Perhaps one of the most controversial easily available chemical relaxants is cannabis (or marijuana). Mere possession of such a substance can present a serious contravention of the law, and thus decisions about its use should not be taken lightly. Ramsay and Compton (2011, p.297), in their chapter in the *Handbook of Schizophrenia Spectrum Disorders*, outline the potential negative psychiatric and psychotropic effects of even short-term use of cannabis.[37] However, there is a growing body of anecdotal evidence available on various blog sites indicating beneficial effects for some individuals affected by autism.[38, 39] Current and on-going research into the action of 'endocannabinoids' (chemicals which occur naturally in the body and which mimic some of the active ingredients in cannabis) is beginning to throw some light onto the question of how cannabis works and the development of medical applications. For example, Jung *et al.* (2012) led a recent study into the effects of cannabis-type chemicals on anxiety and cognitive processes in Fragile-X Syndrome, a common cause of autistic features in individuals.[40]

Animal Assisted Therapy

For those spectrum clients who are not averse to experiencing close contact with animals, the use of domesticated and trained animals to aid relaxation can be of major benefit. Shapiro and Sprague (2009, p.130) state that, 'Virtually any pet, even a goldfish, seems to help in relaxation and stress reduction'.[41] They note that, of course, ownership of an animal in a domestic environment can actively increase stress if supervision is lacking. Sams, Fortney and Willenbring (2006) commented on the usefulness of animals as therapeutic aids on the autism spectrum.[42] They observe that, for the children involved in their study, being with animals that could be petted, stroked or played with brought about significant positive benefits for socialisation, communication and lowered arousal (relaxation). These improvements lay behind the increasing provision of 'assistance dogs' for some people with autism, whereby a dog is trained specifically to take control when, for example, a child displays acute anxiety. Merope Pavlides (2008, pp.31–33) provides a rationale for the use of assistance dogs which includes 'sensory integration and calming'.[43]

Chapter 4

Social Coaching

For most people, being at the centre of a robust and supportive network is critical for emotional and psychological wellbeing. Within such networks we derive important benefits, such as acceptance, acknowledgement, affirmation, affection, companionship and a sense of 'belonging'. Socially typical individuals have an innate, intuitive and instinctive capacity for social development, and therefore find it easy to create and maintain effective relationships. This is not the case for a very large proportion of the autism spectrum population. Here, social confidence and performance can be affected by anxiety. Isolation and withdrawal is often a defensive strategy employed in reaction to this anxiety (or, indeed, to the sense of rejection and conflict that people with autism often experience within their social environments), and it is this isolation and withdrawal which can trigger depression and loneliness. It is therefore useful to consider ways of supporting the development of a functioning social network for a person with autism.

A key element in building a more positive social profile is social coaching. Some counsellors and professional bodies are not happy with the idea of 'directive counselling' and prefer to enable individuals to find their own answers within themselves. However, it is worth noting that many people with autism spectrum conditions genuinely do not know what to do in particular social situations. If that is the case, then the individual will find it difficult to generate his or her own answers from within. Inevitably, this will bring the counsellor into the potential role of mentor or coach. If the practitioner is uncomfortable with this, then professional boundaries can be maintained by referring the spectrum client to someone who can fulfil the coaching role. I have found that combining a counselling and coaching role is useful integrative practice for a number of clients.

I have noted elsewhere that an individual on the autism spectrum will often have difficulty in processing enough social information from an environment to inform appropriate social behaviour.[44] This can apply on both a micro and a macro level. A micro-level difficulty might be an inability to accurately process the full range of facial expressions and gestures used by other people. A macro-level difficulty might arise where an individual shuts down the social processing system after experiencing high levels of anxiety in an environment that contains too many people. Other high-demand situations that can lead to social anxiety include job interviews and financial welfare assessments – some verbal clients have reported becoming mute in such circumstances. Such things can affect self-esteem and confidence. Successful coaching can point individuals to useful social information in their environments, enabling them to build a more positive relationship profile.

To discover where an individual on the autism spectrum might need support socially, it is helpful to facilitate some kind of assessment. Often this will be done by the practitioner, and there are several examples of formal social skills assessment tools available. Chris White (2006) provides The Social Play Record,[45] which aims to assess and develop social play in children with an autism spectrum condition. Moat (2008) presents the AS:SIST Social Assessment Tool for Asperger Syndrome,[46] which can be used with adults as well as children. AS:SIST is an acronym – Asperger Syndrome: Social Integration Skills Training.

Michelle Garcia Winner (2002) produced a more informal Assessment of Social Cognition which features an interesting 'double interview' process[47] – a two-way process in which both the practitioner and the student interview each other. Many therapists become skilled at informally assessing clients through conversation and observation. Nancy J. Patrick (2008) provides a self-assessment process for teenagers and adults with Asperger Syndrome[48] – this can provide the individual with useful self-awareness. Whatever assessment process is carried out, the conclusions can be discussed and pointers for effective intervention can be identified.

Within my clinic, spectrum clients presenting with social anxiety or difficulties with social behaviours may be shown a series of pictures of groups of people engaged in various social activities. If the client uses social language to describe the pictures (such as talking about the potential relationships between the people in the picture), then it demonstrates at least a partial ability to detect social information. An absence of social language in the descriptions might point to an inability to naturally detect that all-important social information. This use of social pictures as part of the assessment process is based on the fact that much neurotypical social behaviour when joining a group is informed by what is already going on within that group. For example, people arriving late to a seminar or workshop will usually take the nearest available seat in an attempt to unobtrusively 'join in' with the behaviour of the already seated delegates. Had they arrived at a break time, they would 'join in' with the more relaxed 'milling around' behaviour of the other delegates around the tea and biscuits. This 'joining in' behaviour is made possible by the ability of the neurotypical person to scan the social environment looking for clues to inform behaviour.

Appropriate coaching can assist the individual in recognising the relevant social information in an environment, and can help the adoption of appropriate behaviour and management strategies in social situations. Social Stories™ and Comic Strip

Conversations are widely used to assist in this kind of process. Carol Gray (1994)[49] first introduced these approaches to the world of autism. They seek to identify to the individual with an autism spectrum condition information about the social environment, including, where possible, the perspectives of other people, and direction about what to do. The Social Stories™ make use of written sentences to build this understanding, although they can be easily illustrated to provide a visual reference. As the name implies, Comic Strip Conversations present similar information in a comic strip format, often using simple line drawings, 'stick' figures and speech and thought bubbles. I have found in my clinic that the use of thought bubbles in a diagram is particularly useful for some clients who have difficulty interpreting the reactions of others.

Simulation and role play can be a further aid in social coaching. These enable the individual to experience how it 'feels' to use the suggested new behaviours, within a safe environment. 'Scripts' can be formulated, which the individual can use outside of the therapeutic environment. For some, the scripts might need to be written down, or perhaps saved as a text file on a mobile device. The scripting can help to reduce the risk that, for some spectrum clients, new information is not flexibly transferred from the learning environment, or therapy room, into real-life situations. Role play is an example of how elements of drama therapy can be incorporated into an integrative approach.

I have found that, for some spectrum clients, it can be difficult to gain a commitment to try out new elements of social behaviour once they have left the counselling room. Work to boost confidence and self-esteem can be useful in such situations. However, in a small number of cases, it has been necessary to arrange for someone to accompany the individual into the target situation so that he or she can practise the new skill. Some people on the autism spectrum are experiential or kinaesthetic learners – in other words, they learn by 'doing'.

When an individual already has the benefit of support worker intervention, then these relationships can be used for such 'mentoring'. Without such opportunities for mentoring, the counsellors may find themselves in the additional role of social worker, and careful thought will need to be paid to therapeutic boundaries. It may be useful in these cases to introduce the client to local support groups and agencies.

Where there are difficulties arising from a client's inability to follow some of the more subtle or abstract social rules, then support around the 'hidden curriculum', as it is often called, will be needed. Grandin and Barron (2005) usefully provide sections on each of The Ten Unwritten Rules of Social Relationships:[50]

- Rules are Not Absolute. They are Situation-based and People-based

- Not Everything is Equally Important in the Grand Scheme of Things

- Everyone in the World Makes Mistakes. It Doesn't Have to Ruin Your Day

- Honesty is Different from Diplomacy

- Being Polite is Appropriate in Any Situation

- Not Everyone Who is Nice to Me is My Friend

- People Act Differently in Public Than They Do in Private

- Know When you're Turning People Off

- 'Fitting In' is Often Tied to Looking and Sounding Like You Fit In

- People are Responsible for Their Own Behaviours.

These were written in recognition of the difficulties experienced by many on the autism spectrum in terms of understanding that, with social norms changing so rapidly, it will never be possible for one individual to master every rule for every situation. They propose the above broad principles that are more likely to apply across ages and across settings.

Couples and Relationship Counselling

There is an increasing prevalence of couples presenting themselves for relationship counselling where at least one partner has high-functioning autism or Asperger Syndrome. One of the potential conflict areas in such relationships is the communicative mismatch. Often the neurotypical partner will complain that everything the Asperger partner says is logically loaded, whilst the Asperger partner will complain that everything the neurotypical partner says is emotionally loaded. Maxine Aston (2003) speaks of a lack of emotional reciprocity in such couples.[51] Helping the couple to bridge this gap will clearly be useful. The counsellor may find him- or herself in something of an educational role while the couple find their feet in terms of understanding each other with a new perspective.

I have often found that couples presenting for this kind of support will have been married for several years (perhaps decades) and typically the Asperger diagnosis has been relatively recent. Some couples have described the sense of relief at finally finding a reason for some of the difficulties they have experienced. However, despite this, for each partner, there is a risk of deep-seated emotional problems remaining as a result of the years of disconnectedness. Sometimes this can be an obstacle for the couple's counselling process, and practitioners may need to be prepared to consider ways of recommending individual therapy for one or other of the partners, either as a parallel or separate process.

In some cases, the neurotypical partner may have been trying to get the Asperger partner into a counselling process for years.

When the relationship is finally presented for therapeutic support, and the Asperger partner engages, it can be a case of 'too little, too late' for the neurotypical partner. The therapeutic process can come to resemble 'divorce management' rather than 'relationship saving', and support might need to be offered to the sometimes bewildered Asperger partner, especially where he or she realises the depth of emotional disconnectedness his or her partner has experienced for many years. Counsellors in this situation (where a process of supporting a couple becomes a process of potentially supporting two individuals) will need to be confident and robust in their understanding of professional boundaries. Some couples in this situation have specifically requested continued individual support from the same therapist, whilst others prefer different counsellors.

Chapter 5

Goals and Targets

Goals and targets are essential elements of approaches such as Cognitive Behavioural Therapy and Neuro-Linguistic Programming. I have commented earlier (in Chapter 2) on the usefulness of both approaches for the field of autism spectrum conditions. CBT certainly fits the cognitive profile of people on the spectrum, and is especially useful where the therapist is aware of the implications of the effects of autism on the individual. Thus, a therapist might use very concrete language and employ visual strategies. The setting of goals and targets will also be an essential part of any life planning process (see Chapter 13). Whilst there are potential difficulties arising from the sole use of such approaches (for example, where clients find their ruminative thinking is made worse, or are left feeling devalued because they perceive that being purely target-focused opens them up to judgement), the sensitive use of goal setting as part of an overall therapeutic package can be extremely successful.

Part of the intrinsic value of goals and targets derives from the observation that many people on the autism spectrum have a different style of executive function compared to the neurotypical population. Paxton and Estay (2007, pp.65–71)[52] give a useful summary of these differences and their implications for things like central coherence (people with autism may have problems getting a sense of the 'whole', or in noticing themes, and making broad interpretations), cognitive flexibility (people with autism tend towards concrete, inflexible thinking), and organisational abilities (some people with autism are extremely disorganised and chaotic; others may be too rigid in their organisation). Differences to the norm in any or all of these areas can lead to conflict within one's environment, and this conflict can create the circumstances for anger, anxiety and feelings of rejection. For example, the weak central coherence practised by many people on the spectrum may lead to the aforementioned failure to glean essential social information from an environment. Cognitive inflexibility can lead to the perception from some neurotypical people that the person with autism is stubborn and egotistic. And organisational difficulties can result in extremely chaotic lifestyles for some (or to the adoption of rigid, routinised patterns). Carefully considered goals and targets help spectrum clients to identify relevant information. They will also help in organising thinking and creating helpful processes.

Goals and targets are easier to set if the client and therapist have a good idea of current circumstances. Motivation to work towards targets is helped if clients feel that these are achievable, and that they have had some involvement in setting them. Vroom (1964) identified a theory of motivation based on expectancy: people are more likely to work towards a goal if they can both see the worth of that goal and that their efforts are likely to be successful.[53]

Charts

The use of charts helps in assessing the current situation and in projecting ahead to the setting of goals. They will also help raise an individual's self-awareness. I have found that charts are often popular with clients with Asperger Syndrome, although motivation to engage with such tools can vary depending, for example, on levels of depression. Pictorial or symbolic charts can be useful for spectrum clients with additional intellectual difficulties in helping them to be more aware of their emotional state.

Mood/behaviour charts are useful in determining frequency of a particular thought, mood or behaviour. Such a chart might be divided into days of the week, with various time slots throughout each day. They can provide a baseline measurement, as well as a monitoring tool once an intervention or strategy is in place. Even without further intervention such charts can lead to positive effects. For example, clients (or their parents and supporting professionals) can often perceive that a mood is pretty much constant. Language used in such cases might consist of the words, 'He is always angry' or 'I'm always anxious'. Providing a simple tick chart can demonstrate that the particular mood or behaviour is actually far less frequent than perceived. This is sometimes enough for the individual or those around him or her to adopt a more relaxed attitude, which might reduce the frequency of occurrence still further. Language used then changes from, 'He's always angry' to 'He's not as angry as we thought he was'. Where the individual notices this, the perception of the mood or behaviour can change from a sense of inevitability to at least consideration of other possibilities. A client may move from feeling like the victim of a mood or behaviour pattern to having some control over it (if only by becoming an observer). This raises the likelihood that suggested interventions or strategies will meet with higher motivation. Where the charts simply provide data, and do not in themselves lead to a reduction in the target mood or behaviour, they can still be used as a baseline measurement.

As well as being used in targeting mood and behaviour reduction, charts can also be useful in assessing things like social and leisure activity, and identifying core beliefs held by individuals that are holding them back. Goals and targets can then be set to help increase particular activities or to change those limiting core beliefs. Gaus (2007) presents the idea of using monthly activity schedules and core belief worksheets (pp.182–193).[54] It can be difficult to shift a spectrum client from their 'all or nothing' thinking just by using traditional 'talking therapy' approaches. Such sessions can deteriorate into intellectual sparring. Charts can provide all-important visual support. They can also help in identifying the process needed to get from the current circumstances to the target situation. I have found that further visual support can derive from the use of flow charts and similar diagrams. These systems assist the spectrum client in terms of task analysis – breaking down a desired aim into achievable steps (or indeed helping the client to understand that his or her stated preferred aim might be unachievable because the intermediate steps simply cannot be met realistically).

Goals need to be specific. It can be difficult to see progress where spectrum clients are simply left with general targets. The statement, 'I need to improve my social skills' or 'I need to get a job' is probably not as helpful as a more specific set of targets that identify what actually needs to be done towards that overall aim. Clients left with overall aims, whilst ostensibly committing to them, can struggle without such clear individual targets. The risk is that they will simply descend further into frustration or depression, and become even less motivated to consider changing behaviour or attitudes. Such a situation can also lead to those around the individual developing a negative perception of the person ('Oh, he'll never achieve much – just look at his record so far'). The result is sometimes that the individual finds him- or herself in a negative, downward spiral, at the centre of a network of people who themselves are negative. This is, indeed, a hopeless situation, and it is difficult for the therapist to identify or generate within the client the motivation to consider change. It is clear that in such situations a spectrum client may not engage with high-level targets (such as 'wouldn't it be great to get a job'), and practitioners must be prepared to limit goal setting to low-level aims (such as simply enabling a client to want to come back next week). In these circumstances, of course, the cumulative effect of achieving low-level targets will be to enable higher goals to be considered.

I have found that it is helpful to assess with spectrum clients (and maybe those around them) their capacity for holding sequential information. Some clients have demonstrated a preference for a 'one-step at a time' approach, often because too much information can overload their processing system. These clients might have difficulty working with a week-long timetable, for instance, and function better with a daily timetable. Others may have a tendency to focus on the end point, without wanting to move through the prior stages. Weekly monitoring and evaluation charts for mood, behaviour or beliefs might need to be adapted in these cases. I have found that a range of charting options is preferable – whilst most clients can cope with a weekly charting system (indeed, some are happy to be given several weeks worth at a time), a number find a daily chart to be more useful. Being aware of a client's capacity for handling sequential information can make a huge difference in motivation to engage with such systems.

Practitioners will sometimes need to assist clients in testing goals, to prevent unrealistic targets being pursued. In NLP parlance, we should be looking for a 'well-formed outcome', which can sit very easily alongside a SMART approach to goal setting (SMART targets are Specific, Measurable, Achievable, Realistic and Timed). A 'well-formed outcome' is helpful for setting a direction of travel (it is a destination), whereas a SMART objective can identify a waypoint on the journey (and clearly there may be several of these). In planning we need the ability to know both where we are headed and which route we are going to take. Testing a well-formed outcome can be achieved through working with the client to produce a list of pros and cons, or utilising tools such as mind-maps. These help to ensure that informed decisions can be made. Having established an end point, and decided upon a route, it will be important to prepare for things going wrong. People on the autism spectrum can handle the unexpected very badly. A range of 'Plan Bs' can be helpful in avoiding such difficulties.

Having positive and realistic goals and targets, together with time scales, can also move clients out of the crisis management cycle. There is a risk that much of the statutory intervention offered to people with autism spectrum conditions is responsive to crisis situations. Short-term, emergency goals are often set, with clients being discharged back into the very situation that triggered the crisis in the first place. Resources may be taken up in the crisis management that could be better placed in looking at longer-term solutions.

Some spectrum clients respond well to discussion of goals for individual sessions. Such discussion can certainly help both therapist and client to avoid prevarication or too much tangential thinking. It can also help to reduce any anxiety that a client feels about a therapeutic session, especially during the early stages of the therapeutic relationship. A current client is assisted to maintain attendance by the reception staff of the clinic, who provide him with an 'agenda' for the forthcoming session. This advance information is agreed between him and myself at the end of the preceding session, and ensures that he attends for the next appointment. Without the information, the client found it extremely difficult even to wait in the waiting room. Now he finds that he can arrive in good time, knowing that he will have something relevant and reassuring to read while he is waiting. An added bonus is that he knows that no-one else will try to talk to him while he is reading – his inability to manage 'small-talk' contributed to his anxiety whilst waiting.

Thus it can be seen that the use of goals and target setting is a useful part of the integrative psychotherapeutic toolkit. Motivation for change is certainly more likely where a client can engage positively with such processes. Even where this is not possible, due perhaps to low intellectual capacity experienced by some people on the autism spectrum, it is useful at least for the therapist to have clear goals in mind.

Chapter 6

Beyond Words

Therapists and counsellors are often looking for ways of establishing contact and rapport with individuals with severe learning and communication difficulties. Straightforward 'talk' therapy alone will not suffice in these situations. There are a number of interventions and approaches that move beyond words and provide a more integrative way of working.

Intensive Interaction

The concept of Intensive Interaction was introduced in Chapter 2. It is an easily learned system that utilises observations of body language and mimicry to enable engagement at a non-verbal level. Phoebe Caldwell[55] and Dave Hewett[56] have been at the forefront of promoting the use of these approaches. Essentially, it operates at a 'pre-verbal' level, and is based on observations of the infant/caregiver interactions that occur well before the infant develops a capacity for words. As such, as well as its usefulness for developing fundamental communication, Intensive Interaction is useful in the development of relationships and in spending pleasurable time with someone. One of the roots of successful intervention using these methods is simple mimicry of whatever the individual is already doing. A child engaged in rocking backwards and forwards whilst sitting on the floor, apparently oblivious to anyone else in the room, may be joined by a therapist (or carer) who sits alongside him or her and copies the movements. An adult with autism might be engaged in obsessively drawing on a piece of paper, to the exclusion of anything else that is going on. A therapist can engage in an interaction simply by taking a piece of paper and mimicking the activity. In both cases, the practitioner shows acceptance of the individual, and of what he or she is doing.

This provides the person with autism with the sense or *feeling* of being accepted, and can often motivate towards a further level of interaction. For example, the practitioner can offer a slight change in the activity to see if the child or adult will mirror back. Where the pair are rocking backwards and forward, the practitioner can experiment with rocking from side to side, to see if the child follows. If the pair are drawing on paper, the practitioner might want to see what happens if he or she offers to draw on the client's piece of paper. This progression from passive co-existence into turn-taking can then lead into the initiation of interactive games and activities. There are usually no verbal prompts, although some interaction pairs may become involved in mirroring vocalisations where necessary. Timing and rhythm are important, and sensitive observation will often inform the practitioner when a change is appropriate.

Feeling accepted and valued is an important aspect of human wellbeing, both psychologically and emotionally, and the value of Intensive Interaction can be seen clearly. The mirroring and sharing of experience is also a key component of building rapport in Neuro-Linguistic Programming, and contributes to the process of 'pacing and leading' – enabling a client to consider progress and change after the therapist has 'walked alongside' for a while, thereby establishing trust. For some spectrum clients, the pacing might involve time for speaking about their favourite subject. The 'leading' might involve setting a timetable for this, allowing the session to move on to other things.

Observation of a client's body language can help to ascertain how he or she feels about what is happening. It is also useful for the practitioner to be self-aware in terms of how he or she is reacting to what a client says or does. This might involve reflection on a thought or feeling that develops during a session. When working non-verbally, the therapist may be aware of bodily sensations that arise, and these are often worth reflecting on. Those inward observations will help the therapist become aware of any transference or counter-transference issues ('Is what I'm feeling a reflection of how the client feels about a significant person in their lives?' or 'Has what I'm feeling been triggered by the client, but actually relates to a significant relationship in my own life?'). Such awareness can also identify projection (a psychological phenomenon in which a person attributes unwanted feelings to another person) and introjection (the internalisation of such projections).

Intensive Therapy

Intensive Interaction is not to be confused with some of the examples of Intensive Therapy available for use with autism spectrum conditions. These include 'Options' (sometimes referred to as the Son-Rise approach), and Applied Behavioural Analysis (ABA – a development of what is sometimes referred to as the Lovaas approach). Interestingly, these approaches are almost diametrically opposed, and yet both claim significant improvements in autistic symptoms. This may be because both systems are essentially child-focused. Whilst Intensive Interaction can easily be delivered alongside other systems in an integrative approach, Intensive Therapy approaches are usually stand-alone interventions, but this should not rule out the use of particular elements as part of an overall therapeutic package.

The Options or Son-Rise approach is ideally delivered by the parents of a child in his or her own home. The approach was developed after the experiences of the Kaufman family (1995) who decided that they were going to 'join' their son in his autistic world, rather than abandon him to it, or enter into conflict with him.[57] It is intensive, and consists of the child's behaviour being imitated (or 'joined'), until the child spontaneously engages in a communicative act (which may simply be head orientation, eye contact, a gesture or a vocalisation). Parents are trained to engage in this kind of interaction. Waiting for the child to lead the interaction provides a sense of acceptance, and enables more complex social interactions to follow. The Son-Rise approach is probably closer to Intensive Interaction than its rival ABA, in its provision of non-confrontational imitation of behaviours to gain communicative development.

In contrast to Son-Rise, the ABA (Applied Behavioural Analysis) approach is one in which the autistic behaviours demonstrated by a child are specifically targeted for extinction. There is also a greater reliance on verbal instruction. ABA developed from the work of Dr Ivar Lovaas (1987),[58] a professor of psychology at the University of California, Los Angeles. He was interested in behaviour modification, and saw autistic behaviours as *barriers* to the development of communication, rather than a potential *catalyst* for social contact. These behaviours were to be removed and replaced with more 'acceptable' behaviour. Early work with children tended to include controversial aversive techniques, although modern ABA programmes are geared towards positive reinforcement. Application of ABA tends to be as intensive as Son-Rise, although parental involvement is diminished by the use of professional workers. School-based ABA programmes are also becoming popular.

There is a lack of objective, comparative research to determine which, if any, of these interventions is most beneficial. It seems that there are some major differences in philosophy between the two, and yet both are able to point to significant improvements for a proportion of children undergoing treatment. ABA would appear to be the more 'measurable' of the two, as it lends itself more to evaluation and review of specific targets (but it is worth noting that measurement of 'compliance' provides little evidence of emotional wellbeing). The Son-Rise approach seems to lean more heavily on anecdotal evidence from families and, indeed, a recent independent study published on the Son-Rise website identified that researchers from Northwestern University, Illinois, only had access to parental questionnaires rather than being able to observe children directly (Jenkins, Schuchard and Thompson 2012).[59] But none of this makes one approach better than the other and, indeed, it may be a false argument. People with autism are individuals and therefore different from each other. It may well be, therefore, that some will respond better to one or the other, and some may even need a mixture of acceptance and guidance – in other words, elements of both approaches.

Sensory Integration Therapy

A further range of non-verbal, or pre-verbal, support for wellbeing on the autism spectrum can be found within elements of Sensory Integration Therapy. Phoebe Caldwell and Jane Horwood (2008) have identified the value of integrating Intensive Interaction with Sensory Integration Therapy.[60] The two approaches often fit side by side. Both Intensive Interaction and sensory integration involve close observation of behaviour. Body language is used to focus attention and provide emotional engagement in Intensive Interaction, whilst in sensory integration approaches, physical sensations can be used to help a child's 'disintegrated' brain to begin making some all-important connections using information from the environment. Sensory observations can also help to explain at least some of the distressing or challenging behaviours that can occur on the autism spectrum. For many people on the spectrum, acute emotional distress can be demonstrated during periods of sensory overload – when input becomes too much for the 'disintegrated' system to handle. Some occupational therapists are recommending 'Sensory Diets'[61] for people with autism, which seek to provide appropriate sensory input for the individual to regulate his or her system. This will include things like the 'sensory relaxers' discussed in Chapter 3. Reducing sensory distress and enabling relaxation in this manner can open the way for more effective social, communicative and emotional exchanges based around Intensive Interaction.

As well as assessing to see if sensory distortions and overload can be diminished through the use of relaxers, tactile toys and substances, touch/pressure and multi-sensory environments, there is also potential value in investigating visual and auditory processing, as well as looking at vestibular and proprioceptive functioning (balance and body awareness, etc.). Many people with autism have reported experiencing distressing visual processing events, with sensory and emotional balance being achieved with the use of, for example, tinted lenses. Examples include Donna Williams (1996, p.62)[62] and Wendy Lawson (1998),[63] who both describe their relief at being prescribed lenses that helped to filter out unwanted light. Olga Bogdashina (2004, p.154) highlights some of the sound sensitivities prevalent on the autism spectrum[64] – distress caused by these difficulties can lead to instances of sensory shutdown, or to the deliberate seeking out of certain stimuli. Bogdashina (2003, p.34) also discusses the use of therapeutic techniques to assist with any issues with proprioception and balance.[65] Movement exercises that involve spinning, jumping, hopping, trampolining, throwing, catching and wriggling are all popular activities helping towards sensory integration. Where there is a risk of over-stimulation, activities such as yoga, Pilates and tai chi can be helpful for some spectrum clients. These disciplines are autism-friendly, in that they involve routine, structure and, in group situations, plenty of space between each participant.

Written and Visual Support

In emotionally volatile situations, or when going over distressing material in a therapeutic session, some clients fail to retain any verbal information that may be offered. This can be because their emotional defensive system shuts down peripheral awareness – it is almost as if they genuinely do not hear what the therapist is saying. In other cases, the spectrum client might have a general delay in processing verbal input, and if too much happens after the session, the information may be lost completely. I have found that writing things down for some clients has proved to be invaluable for retention. One current client likes to write everything down for himself (I have to factor this in to the session time). Another is happy for relevant notes to be supplied via e-mail after each session.

I have also found that for some spectrum clients who have difficulty processing their emotional reactions, the drawing of cartoons, diagrams and simple stick-man pictures can help them externalise their feelings. It provides an opportunity for dissociation or detachment (which are common, natural defence mechanisms), and creates a 'safe external space' for discussing experiences and feelings that are too distressing when left internally. Such an approach needs to be used with caution where a client displays a pathological degree of dissociation from reality (although the value of using fantasy will be discussed in Chapter 9). No particular drawing talent is needed for these ideas – it will suffice for both therapist and client to recognise the concepts and representations being drawn. One current client uses drawings himself to put across some of his feelings, and will often prepare for a session by sketching out some of the key concepts he wishes to cover. Further ideas around using creativity in therapy are discussed in the next chapter.

Chapter 7

Using Play and Creativity in Therapy

'Play' is an important part of physical, social and emotional development in children. It helps to prepare for meeting societal demands and roles. It supports the development of personality and attachments. It has a functional aspect, in terms of learning how the world works. It teaches about turn-taking and sharing, negotiation and compromise. It boosts the development and use of imagination. It enables self-realisation. It helps to prepare for adult life. And, above all, it is fun!

It is commonly stated that many children on the autism spectrum have difficulty with the sensory and social aspects of play. This does not have to mean that they do not want to engage in play – Wendy Usher (2012) cites research conducted by Autism Bedfordshire (a UK support organisation) which identified that the children with autism who were consulted wanted to play, but did not know how to join in; some were happy with solo play; and some reported mutual enjoyment when with others who wanted to engage in similar activities.[66] Inclusive play schemes, aimed at children with autism, can be very successful in enabling interactive play. For some spectrum children, their social isolation may be significant enough to warrant specialist individual intervention. A play therapist might work with the child, or a group of children, to actively teach play skills. The therapeutic use of play can also, of course, enable children of any neurological perspective to work through emotional issues. This can extend to the use of creative approaches to therapeutic intervention.

Active Teaching of Play Skills

Whilst not necessarily seen as part of an integrative psychotherapeutic repertoire, the teaching of play skills can open up to a child (or indeed adult with autism – see below) elements of social and emotional reciprocity that were previously unavailable. The ability to effectively communicate emotional states and reactions is essential in maintaining emotional balance and wellbeing. For many observers, a child's first play 'object' is an adult (see, for example, Beyer and Gammeltoft 2000, p.45).[67] The adult provides opportunities for mimicry of sounds, gestures and facial expression. Children then expand their range of play objects (which will include toys, games and other human beings). Where this early mimicry has not been possible due to developmental delay, for example, it may be possible to kick-start the process through the introduction of Intensive Interaction approaches. Observation of the child's natural preferences will be important. Play work in general needs to be structured in a way that is relevant and motivating for the client. There will be clear advantages in using those concepts that individuals are known to be interested in.

Sensorimotor play is the second major play milestone. In non-autistic children, this would normally occur alongside further interactions with caregivers. We might expect to see the beginnings of 'joint attention' at this stage – say, six to eight months of age. Sensorimotor play is characterised by exploring the taste, texture and smell of objects. The child might experiment with how the object moves. It is worth noting that some people with autism retain elements of this sensorimotor exploration well into adult life. They can continue to navigate an environment through the use of their physical senses. This may be a reflection that individuals have become 'stuck' at that stage of development, and may need support (where considered appropriate) to move through it into higher-level interactions with their environments.

In typical development, organising play begins around the age of six months, and is fully operational by around nine or ten months. Here, children will begin to stack toys, line them up, and put them inside each other. The actual purpose of the toys is incidental in the early stages. The organisation activity seems to be driven by a desire to see how things fit together. The child's awareness has expanded from the object in his or her hand, to examining the relationship between that object and others. There is a developing sense of control over one's environment. Perhaps this explains why for some children on the autism spectrum the need to arrange objects in exact relationship to each other remains so important well on into childhood, and perhaps even into adulthood. Having this sense of control and therefore security is emotionally very satisfying, and for a child, or adult, with no sense of social control it can be very attractive. If this explanation is accepted, then practitioners will recognise this obsessional organisational behaviour as a defence mechanism. Again, such knowledge should inform therapists that they should be sensitive to causing further emotional distress. If we simply seek to remove the obsessional behaviour we risk exposing the individual to unmitigated stress, which can drive even more defensive behaviour. Support for play here might involve enabling the obsessional arrangements to become part of an interactive game, thus bringing social interaction into the 'safe' realm. For example, I have enjoyed many an hour playing old-fashioned games like 'KerPlunk', 'Jenga' and 'Connect 4' with spectrum clients of all ages.

Functional play becomes a major feature of activity around 9 to 12 months, and typically accompanies major leaps in shared attention. Toys and objects are used intentionally, after their proper purpose. Children will often imitate the object-related behaviour of other people. For example, a child might 'help' Mum to type an e-mail, or will draw over a wall in an attempt to copy Dad who has just been filling in a crossword. Early dialogue might begin around this time. For the spectrum child, any atypical relationship with the social environment might mean less opportunity to 'notice' what other people are doing. This could explain the potential difficulties that a child with autism might have in picking up functional play. And if autistic children *do* develop a significant level of functional play, it may simply be because they have worked it out for themselves. A child, or adult, needing support in this area can be helped by providing specific opportunities for observation and 'noticing' others. The child may have no natural instinct for such activity, and so a parent or practitioner might need to find ways of gaining the child's attention. The family of one current client use favourite action figures to ensure that the child looks in the right direction.

From about 18 months onwards, typically developing children begin to use pretend play. They are beginning to make 'representations' in their mind. This can take several forms. 'Object replacement' involves substitution of one object for another. For example, a 'Duplo' brick might be used as a car. 'Projection' of certain qualities might enable the pretence that a doll is alive. The child is beginning to explore the use of imagination, and uses that imagination to predict and try to influence what other people are thinking ('Shh! The dolly is asleep.'). This awareness of what other people might have on their minds and in their hearts typically develops into full-blown empathy. Pretend play could be said to be an apprenticeship for adult social behaviour and it is such a fundamental element that it needs to be 'wired' or integrated very early.

It is widely accepted that many children with autism spectrum conditions do not demonstrate pretend play, if at all, in the same way as other children. Where it occurs, it often tends to be dominated by special interests or obsessional repetition.

If it is accepted that pretend play influences the development of empathy and adult social behaviour, it follows that any difficulty in this area is likely to lead to social adjustment issues. Given that effective emotional expression is usually enabled by well-functioning social relationships, it can be seen that attempts to kick-start or improve the experience of pretence (or the development of empathy) may well help people with autism with their emotional regulation. Structured play with a partner might enable the person with autism to develop a concept of pretence, especially if he or she is directed to observe, and ultimately experience, part of the play. The use of dolls and puppets may be helpful here, as might using technology to provide virtual examples of pretence. An example of this is provided by Herrera and colleagues (2008), who published a case study pointing to the success of virtual reality techniques for teaching pretend play.[68]

Puppet Play

The use of puppets is becoming increasingly popular in play therapy settings. It is one of the ways that spectrum clients can be enabled to learn about emotional recognition and response. Puppets can be used to act out emotional scenarios – either by the child or the practitioner. Real-life emotional situations can be intimidating to a person with autism – puppets help in providing opportunities for safe observation and exploration. I have used puppets to practise conversation, to develop stories and to enable spectrum clients to examine the thoughts, feelings and reactions of other people. In doing this, I have noticed that some clients seem to disclose more information about their own feelings through these 'third-party' interactions. This is another example of providing the opportunity for 'externalisation' of feelings that are too difficult to face internally.

Creative Approaches

Music, art and drama therapy can all provide excellent opportunities for the exploration of emotional content. Elements of each of these can form part of an integrative psychotherapeutic approach. Therapists can allow a child or adult to explore musical instruments in a room, noticing what he or she is drawn to, and then can use those items to establish interaction. The natural rhythm of the child can be observed, mirrored and paced. The child can be allowed to lead. The therapist might initiate a new rhythm, to see if the child will follow. Musical 'conversations' can take place, teaching the child about the rhythm, flow and turn-taking elements of interaction. Group situations can be utilised for further exploration.

Sessions that include an element of art can also be helpful in exploring interaction, emotional expression and communication. People with autism frequently lack the kind of imagination that leads to original drawing, and thus much autistic art tends to be idiosyncratic – a child might always draw the same object; some adults with autism draw in a very immature way. Not all will readily engage with an opportunity to draw, but where a spectrum client is motivated, practitioners can explore mirroring, co-operation and interactive working. Practitioners should be sensitive to the client's sense of personal space to avoid 'invading'.

The use of drama in therapeutic sessions can enable clients to externalise difficult emotional processes. Role play (using people, or dolls, for example) can enable people with autism to explore other people's emotions and reactions. It can also help them to rehearse what has been suggested in social coaching. Clients can be involved in the role playing, or they can simply observe (the therapist might act as a commentator here).

The value of using exercise and movement in supporting balance and proprioception was presented in Chapter 6, as part of a discussion around sensory integration. Drama work can be successfully combined with the creative use of music and movement to further enhance improvements in sensory processing. This can be more attractive to adult clients who may find the idea more age-appropriate than engaging in 'play therapy'. Two of my recent clients have so valued this kind of experience that they have enrolled for formal dance classes. They find the structure helpful, as well having as the opportunity to explore proximity and touch. Another useful application of music and movement techniques involves the possibility of using attunement techniques. These start with mirroring, and develop into situations where the practitioner can reflect the clients' movement back to them in a slightly exaggerated way. This can improve the clients' awareness of their own movement, as well as opening up pathways for interactive exchanges. Attunement work can also give scope to help the client develop alternative movement patterns, aiding sensory integration.

Chapter 8

Hypnotherapeutic Techniques

A hypnotic state is one in which an individual is relaxed, and able to direct additional specific focus whilst peripheral awareness is reduced. It has very little to do with being asleep or unconscious – people undergoing hypnosis are very aware of what is happening. Hypnotherapists make use of the relaxed, focused state to offer suggestions to the client – sometimes directing the formation of an image or helping to increase motivation for a change in behaviour or perception.

The *British Medical Journal* (1999)[69] and the British Psychological Society (2001)[70] have published reports stating the effectiveness of hypnotic procedures in pain management, relaxation, anxiety management, treating insomnia, phobia extinction, irritable bowel syndrome, weight loss and psychosomatic illness. Michael Yapko (2006) has written extensively on the value of hypnosis for treating depression.[71] Any of these conditions and needs may be seen across the autism spectrum, and therefore it is worth considering whether hypnosis may be a valuable tool for integrative psychotherapeutic intervention with spectrum clients. It is perhaps worth noting here that interest is growing in the innate ability of some people with autism to enter a 'trance-like' (or hypnotic state) without external intervention (or induction, as it is referred to amongst hypnotherapists). Bogdashina (2010, p.169) has noted the way in which some people on the spectrum '…rescue themselves from overload by escaping to an entertaining, secure and hypnotic level of hyper-sensation'.[72] Donna Williams (1998, p.45) talks of 'resonance' with objects – getting hypnotically lost in them.[73] These examples provide further reasons to consider hypnotherapy as part of the treatment profile for spectrum clients.

Ethical considerations are as important with hypnotherapy as with any other intervention. Consent is of particular importance – in my own practice, I will not offer hypnotherapy unless I feel satisfied that I have the express informed consent of my client. This is very difficult to obtain from someone with a severe learning disability. No matter how 'hypnotic' his or her own behaviour appears, it is important to avoid the assumption that the person will 'consent' to external induction. This is not to say that a therapist should not seek to 'join' the client in his or her fascination, either with a view to establishing contact, or to 'lead' the client to a different state. This is, after all, the philosophy behind Intensive Interaction. And neither is it to say that the therapist cannot offer parents advice around the use of hypnotic CDs at home – perhaps to assist a child in going to sleep. Some spectrum clients refer themselves for hypnotherapy. In these cases I provide a thorough explanation of the process, and offer a 'taster' which usually involves a relaxation exercise.

Specific literature around hypnosis and autism is sparse. It is an under-researched area of practice. However, there is some useful information contained in the observations from the practice of Diane Yapko (2006), who writes about the '*utilization approach*' to treating depression on the autism spectrum,[74] and Dawn Heather (2011), who is a specialist practitioner for people with Asperger Syndrome.[75] The 'utilization approach' refers simply to adapting one's approach to the interests and values of the client. In the context of Asperger Syndrome, this would mean identifying the interests and processing style of the individual, and using these within the hypnotherapeutic intervention.

Future Progression

Hypnotherapy can be combined with elements of Cognitive Behavioural Therapy and Neuro-Linguistic Programming, particularly in terms of goal setting and the use of visualisation. Some people with autism spectrum conditions have a default visual processing style. Temple Grandin (1996, p.19) speaks of translating words into movies, which run like a video in her head.[76] Where this visual processing is prevalent, I have found it helpful to get spectrum clients to visualise themselves at the point of achieving their goal (perhaps running the 'video' through to the end point). This is similar to the NLP technique of 'future pacing' – getting clients to 'connect' with how they will actually feel at the point of achievement. The question is often asked, 'What do you want?', followed by the supplementary question, 'How will it feel when you get there?'

Many people will associate hypnotherapy with regression, but there is just as much value, if not more, in getting clients to look ahead positively. This is sometimes called 'progression' work. Because the projected situation has not happened yet, and is currently 'unreal', it requires an imaginative process to take place. Hypnosis can simultaneously create the circumstances in which these visualisations can happen, and accelerate the process of absorbing the concept of a positive future. Clients with a *past orientation* use the past as a reference point for decision making. Hence negative experience (or the perception of negative experience) can decrease motivation to engage with considering positive futures. I have seen spectrum clients who continually relate past negative experiences when we attempt to construct their 'time-line' (the story so far). This is also seen in some presentations of depression in the neurotypical population. Where a spectrum client is depressed, the past orientation can become a real barrier to progress in therapy, and positive future visualisation becomes a major asset in the practitioner's toolkit. If a client is a visual thinker, and yet has difficulty in generating an image of a positive future, it can be useful to return to the time-line to identify actual positive memories. The client can be assisted to identify with the feelings during that event, so that they can be projected ahead and associated with future success. Where another modality forms the default processing style (for example, auditory thinking), then this modality needs to be woven into the hypnotic projection. The therapist can invite clients to focus specifically on the words being used in the hypnotic session, or to imagine what people will say to them when they achieve their goal.

I have noticed that even where future progression proves unsuccessful, creating a new perception (reframing) of a negative time-line can be very helpful. Here the therapist simply acknowledges the negative events highlighted by the client, but creates therapeutic space between them for the insertion of positive memories. It is useful to translate this into an actual diagram for clients to take away with them.

Metaphor

'Metaphor' in hypnosis is really nothing more than therapeutic story-telling, and it is often used to explore situations and possibilities. With many spectrum clients having a concrete cognitive style, the use of metaphor needs to be carefully considered. Whilst I have noticed that some people on the autism spectrum show more flexibility of thought in hypnosis compared to 'normal' awareness, I still tend to base any metaphors on the expressed interests of the individual. This ensures that the individual has a better chance of maintaining focus on the content of the session. It has sometimes proved useful to talk about dreams and day-dreams to spectrum clients as a way of introducing them to the concept of metaphor. On occasion I will invite clients to continue the metaphor themselves. This enables the assessment of how powerfully they can engage with, for example, the concept of a positive future. It can also identify whether the ruminative or perseverative client continues that thinking whilst in hypnosis. Where this proves to be the case, the therapist can present alternative perspectives, and offer suggestions for taking the thought process in a new direction.

Anchoring

The use of 'anchors' is a technique shared between NLP and hypnotherapy. An anchor is a very effective strategy for maintaining or recreating a desired state and, of course, is most effective if a client can use it outside of the therapy setting. An anchor can be created to enable swift relaxation, to deal with anxiety-provoking situations or to remind clients of a particular goal. For example, a client can be induced to experience a very relaxed state and the therapist will use suggestions to help him or her to identify with that state using all the senses. I tend to ask clients to imagine, picture or remember their favourite place – a safe space or a place where they feel most comfortable. This can be 'anchored' to a particular word, image or sensation (depending on the default processing modality present), with the suggestion that the client actively thinks of the anchor (or trigger) whenever it is needed. For clients needing a more concrete anchor, I usually ask them to choose a glass pebble from a dish on my desk. When the ideal place of relaxation is reached, or when the image of the safe place is created, I tell them to grip the pebble tightly in their hand to make an association between the feeling and the pebble. It is then relatively easy to suggest that the pebble can be slipped into a pocket or handbag, where it remains available as a concrete reminder of the sensation. Alternative anchors include associating the relaxation, safe space or goal with the kinaesthetic action of lightly gripping the palm of one hand between the thumb and forefinger of the other hand, or with touching a wristwatch or ring.

To test the association, most hypnotherapists 'peak' the experience by building it up as high as possible in terms of sensation. A complete change of focus is then implemented, perhaps by asking the individual to recite his or her phone number backwards. The client is then asked to use the anchor to see how quickly, and to what level of intensity, the required feeling is recreated.

Where clients are sceptical of the usefulness of an anchor, I remind them how easily their negative associations can be triggered. It logically follows that positive associations can be targeted and implemented, even if we have to work at them.

Control Room Technique

The idea of using the mind as a literal 'nerve centre' or control room is a classic hypnotherapeutic technique, used in all kinds of situations where sensitivity is problematic. There can be advantages in using such a concept in cases of hyper- or hypo-sensitivity, hyper-vigilance or where pain management, obsessional behaviours or chaotic functioning are features of an individual's presentation. Where this method is used, the therapist offers the suggestion that the mind can operate as a control room. An image of various dials, levers, switches and gauges is introduced, alongside the possibility that each can be turned up or down according to personal preference. Each dial can be given a label if necessary. If spectrum clients have difficulty in generating a suitable image, I will often show them photographs to provide a starting point.

Dialogue Work

Where clients experience particular difficulties with significant relationships, or there is confusion about other people's reactions, I often suggest using dialogue in hypnosis. This technique revolves around asking clients to recall actual interactions, or to imagine hypothetical conversations (easier if one is actually scheduled and causing anxiety). In hypnosis, clients are asked to state what they would like to say to the person (or people) concerned. They are then asked one of two things. I will either ask them to state what they think the other person will answer (in which case we can examine the reasons for that, or for potential alternative answers) or I will suggest that they can actually become the other person for a while, to see if they can imagine the other person's thoughts and feelings. The latter is traditionally held to be difficult for spectrum clients to do, on the grounds of poor empathic skills. However, I have noticed that specific, targeted empathy such as that within the dialogue technique is often possible. If it appears that clients need an advocate in their significant interactions with other people, rehearsal of this nature can help to provide an 'inner advocate', especially if combined with an anchor. Clients who demonstrate fearfulness in therapeutic dialogue situations may need the suggestion of an actual helper within the hypnosis. I might try to get clients to picture themselves as a child in the scene, and introduce a confident, adult version of themselves to offer comfort and protection, thus creating the idea of being able to use one's own inner resources.

Cinema Screen/SWISH Technique

This is another approach shared between NLP and hypnotherapy. It is particularly useful when dealing with stressful or anxiety-provoking situations that need rapid resolution. The visual nature of the technique makes it ideal for the autism spectrum. Clients should be warned that the approach starts with the generation of a sharp and focused image of the stressful situation, but that is the whole point of the exercise – to teach a new way of reacting that does not lead to panic or 'shut-down'. The image of the stressful situation should not be difficult to picture – it is likely to be a feature of everyday life. Once the negative trigger has been identified, the therapist will ask the client to describe a positive replacement image: 'How would you like to feel?' or 'What would it be like if you could deal with this successfully?' The client will be asked to describe this albeit hypothetical situation in as much detail as possible.

The technique relies on the interchange of the two images. Clients are asked to picture the negative scenario as if it was on a huge screen. Ideally, they will be asked to imagine the physical sensations that are associated with it. This image is then put to one side – for clients who have difficulty with imagination, it might be possible to suggest that the screen is actually a giant swipe screen (like those seen on tablet computers). Once swiped, the image is replaced with the positive scenario – ideally, the client should be encouraged to make this as vivid as possible.

This time, the image is shrunk to a postage stamp size in one corner of the screen, and should become black and white, whilst the original negative image is recreated. The focus on the negative image should be intense enough for the client to begin to feel uncomfortable, at which point, the SWISH point is reached – simply allow the images to swap rapidly, so that the positive image becomes dominant, and colourful, whilst the negative one recedes into a corner, becoming monochrome. When the client is comfortable with the positive image, and has enjoyed it for a while, it is usual to generate a neutral image, before repeating the SWISH process once again. This can be repeated for as long as is necessary, with the suggestion that the client can practise this outside of the therapy room.

Boosting Self-esteem and Enhancing Performance

Spectrum clients often present with low self-esteem, and exhibit anxiety regarding forthcoming social interaction opportunities (whether formal or informal). One hypnotic system that can be helpful in these areas is a combination of self-hypnosis training and auto-suggestion. Auto-suggestion was pioneered by Émile

Coué (1857–1926), who coined the commonly used self-help phrase: 'Every day, in every way, I am getting better and better'.[77] This, and statements like it, can be repeated whilst in hypnosis, and there are clear advantages in teaching self-hypnosis to clients in order for them to be able to continue using the phrases outside of the counselling room. Practising the statements over several days can boost clients' sense of self-worth, and consequently their confidence about managing social situations.

Where a client is sceptical about the value of such statements, or is self-conscious about repeating them, I often employ Newton's Third Law of Motion: 'To every action there is an equal and opposite reaction'. I observe to the client that we are both sitting in a chair, in equilibrium. The downward force of gravity on our bodies is met by the upward force exerted by the chair, with the result that 'we are sitting comfortably'. I translate this into looking at the forces exerted by the things that we hear. We allow the 'force' of repeated negative statements to influence us – we start to believe them, and then we start to repeat them in our self-talk. It is possible that exposure to statements like, 'There's something wrong with Johnny' can eventually be transposed to the self-statement, 'I'll never amount to much.' Without at least an equal and opposite force, our emotional equilibrium is lost, and we begin a downward spiral into depression, poor self-esteem and low motivation. Positive self-statements can provide that opposite force.

An alternative hypnotic approach for boosting self-esteem utilises the ego-strengthening theories of Milton Erickson (1901–1980). Erickson would make use of a client's previous experience of achievement, or feeling good about themselves, and would try to recreate this sensation during hypnosis (Frederick and McNeal 1998). This can then be linked to a current situation or a future event. Providing an anchor can further enhance this process – I might invite clients to deepen their sensation of feeling good, and then apply the anchor (see 'Anchoring' above).

Chapter 9

Imagery and Story-making

Imagery and stories can form a useful part of many of the approaches already discussed. NLP and hypnotherapy are obvious examples of interventions that employ visualisation. 'Stories' are sometimes used as elements of hypnotherapy and play therapy, and storyboards as part of drama therapy. Combining story-making and imagery allows for the safe exploration of difficult emotional material, and we have already seen how the use of Social Stories™ can be used to enhance social coaching. Pictures can be added to charts and diagrams to assist the consideration of goals in CBT. This chapter will focus on ways of introducing and using stories and imagery with spectrum clients.

As early as Chapter 1 it was pointed out that many people on the autism spectrum are visual thinkers, and we have seen examples of how some spectrum clients translate the spoken word into visual images (see Chapter 8). It is clear that, for these individuals, the therapeutic use of imagery can open useful pathways for progress. Where clients already have a natural capacity for running 'video' or 'movies' in their heads, then there may be a preference for working with flowing or moving images. Some clients are happier to work with single images, or 'stills', and where these are difficult to generate internally I have found it helpful to provide external pictures to look at and discuss (or recall during a hypnotic session). Peaceful, soothing images can be used to enhance relaxation work. It should be remembered that for some individuals on the autism spectrum, their 'soothing' images might be very different to those of a neurotypical orientation. It is worth emphasising again the value of making an assessment of the spectrum client's range of interests.

Many people on the autism spectrum experience transitional anxiety. This may be on a macro or micro level. At a micro level, anxiety may be demonstrated when simply changing activities, or moving from room to room. A macro-level transition might be seen when changing schools. These kinds of anxiety will often be due to a lack of information about what is going to happen, or about what is expected. The benefits of providing visual images in timetables for some individuals with autism have been widely reported. One of the central tenets of the TEACCH approach (Treatment and Education of Autistic and related Communication handicapped CHildren)[78] involves structured teaching for both children and adults, with a heavy emphasis on visual communication strategies. These provide individuals with enough information about their environments and timetables, in formats designed to aid quick and easy processing, to assuage much of the anxiety. Combining this approach with, for example, Social Stories™, can be even more powerful in enabling anxiety-free transitions.

Storyboards

These processes can be taken still further with the use of transitional storyboards. Directors of animated films will be familiar with this concept – the provision of a sequence of pictures to provide an outline of the story to be told. As well as being useful for timetabling, or programming, picture sequences can be very useful in preparing people with autism for major transitions. For example, advance images can be obtained of a new environment and incorporated into a sequential, virtual 'journey' around the premises.

A more advanced therapeutic use of storyboards can be offered to spectrum clients experiencing depression, if they have difficulty engaging with imagery in hypnosis. Time-line work was mentioned in Chapter 8 – storyboards can be created to provide an external visual reference. Clients can be encouraged to relate their 'story' so far, and therapists can enable the continuation of this process in an attempt to consider a potential positive future. A further advantage of this mode of working is that it allows for effective planning towards achieving the goal. If the storyboard reveals a predominantly negative overview, individuals can be encouraged to make space between some of the images for the insertion of positive memories, thereby providing a positive 'reframe'. Storyboards can also provide an essential perspective on causal links between events, and between those events and people's reactions.

Story-making

Spectrum clients will occasionally have difficulty in managing specific strong emotions. This might occur when memories are triggered during therapy, or when other work enables the lifting of defence mechanisms that have been engaged in suppressing emotions. In therapeutic parlance, the release of unconscious material is sometimes referred to as an 'abreaction'. Whilst this can be cathartic for many neurotypical clients, and some spectrum clients, I have noticed that such emotional processing can be traumatic for a number of people with autism. Work leading up to the release of strong emotions needs to include discussion and assessment of how the individual processes and deals with 'normal' emotionality. If it is suspected that the process will be too intimidating, the use of story-making can be extremely beneficial.

When working with children, it is usually quite easy to begin a process of story-making. Most children, even those with autism, will be familiar with stories. Many have favourites – this is often a good place to start with spectrum children. I have invited children to recreate a favourite story, and followed this up by doing an exercise in imagining themselves to be part of the story, perhaps as an observer, or by replacing one of the characters. We can then develop new storylines which might feature some of the difficulties they are having in real life, utilising other characters in the story to offer solutions. A key development is to use a new storyline where one of the other characters experiences the life problem, and the client's character offers the solution. This kind of work places the child in control, and enables him or her to realise that problem-solving is not only possible, but useful. The use of puppets, dolls, toy figures, etc., can assist the whole story-making process.

Similar work with spectrum adults is also possible. It may, of course, be some time since they experienced a good story – it is often the case that spectrum adults have actively avoided fictional stories in preference for factual or scientific literature. If they can recall stories from childhood it will provide a place to start. Where there is a reluctance to engage with fiction, I have found it useful to identify historical or topical people whose life stories are well known. It has sometimes proved possible to create stories using these characters' lives, following the same format as used with children. Here it is possible to intersperse the storylines with the emotional scenarios that can cause the client problems in real life. This externalisation (or therapeutic displacement or dissociation) can enable in-depth exploration in a safe and controlled way.

Stories can also be used to elicit a client's feelings about family members or other significant people. Characters in a well-known story can be replaced by people from the client's real-life network. This can be a way of assessing how the individual sees members of his or her network, as well as being a method of enabling the client to see other people's perspectives. With both children and adults with autism I have experimented with creating completely original stories where the characters are drawn from the real-life network. However the story is constructed, it can be useful, where possible, to enable clients to relax, and imagine a film being made of the story, where they take the role of director (even if they feature as a character in the story). This is to give individuals the experience of exercising some control over particular aspects of their lives that they otherwise feel are outside of their influence. Adding storyboards to this combination of story and imagery can make the whole process extraordinarily powerful for some individuals.

Guided Affective Imagery

Guided Affective Imagery (GAI) was introduced effectively into the therapeutic toolkit by Hanscarl Leuner (1918–1996). He became interested in the symbolic imagery within dreams and day-dreams, and found that induced day-dreams offered a powerful therapeutic outlet. It is the symbolism that differentiates these kind of interventions from straightforward visualisation. Leuner's ideas were encapsulated in his paper published in the *American Journal of Psychotherapy* (1969).[79] I have successfully used elements of his approach with spectrum clients, particularly those with Asperger Syndrome.

To gauge the suitability of GAI with clients, the therapist simply asks them to relax into a chair, or couch, and picture in their mind's eye a flower. The client describes the flower, in answer to questions posed by the therapist. Some clients realise that the flower is something to do with themselves – in other words they can appreciate the symbolism. It is these clients for whom GAI can be most effective. Guided day-dreams (the use of active imagination) can follow over subsequent sessions, each following a different theme, but all relying on the client to recount what he or she sees. Classic GAI scenarios include meadows, mountains, streams and houses. Each can provide a client who has Asperger Syndrome with important messages about hir or her life and circumstances. Even the lack of an image can be useful – the therapist might ask someone who describes being able to see only darkness when they close their eyes, '…and describe the darkness…the temperature…the texture…'

I have found that allowing clients to interpret for themselves what the symbolism means is very useful. My own interpretations are neurotypical and therefore potentially unhelpful. Even if I were a therapist on the autism spectrum, my interpretations would still be my own. The practitioner plays the role of calm observer, intervening where necessary with safe suggestions to develop the story further. If a client becomes distressed, then the therapist can suggest use of a 'safe space', or that the image can begin to diminish into the distance. GAI should not be utilised for clients who may find the symbolism to be overwhelming.

Example of a Multiple Creative Approach – Ellie's Island

Ellie (not her real name) is a woman with Asperger Syndrome in her thirties who has used various opportunities for counselling and psychotherapy over a number of years. She came to see me after a period of time in conflict with family members. I present this brief case history as an example of how visual story work can provide a key for unlocking emotional content.

Ellie and I explored her situation together, using various story scenarios. Ellie recalled liking stories in her childhood that involved travel and exploration, and was particularly fascinated by the voyages of discovery undertaken by people such as Christopher Columbus, Vasco da Gama and James Cook. As we talked, I learned that she liked stories about previously uncharted islands. Several sessions were taken up with discussion of island exploration. I felt that we were becoming bogged down in this, and that Ellie was perseverating whilst trying to avoid talking about the family conflicts that had brought her to therapy in the first place. I asked her in one session to sit back in her chair and imagine being an explorer herself, writing in a journal the tale of discovering a new island. Unsurprisingly, her story followed the lines of some of those she had read in childhood. I asked her to imagine walking around the island, meeting members of the family one by one, hoping to see if she could picture the dialogues that would take place. Ellie did not want to engage in this process – she did not want people she was in conflict with to 'spoil' her island. She felt that having to focus on and confront these people would cause her to lose the image of the island.

I suggested that we draw the island, to provide an external and tangible image for her. Ellie proved to be quite skilled as an artist, and successfully drew a detailed outline of an island, complete with streams, hills and vegetation. I asked her to locate herself on the island, but she said that she didn't want to be in one place – she wanted to move around the island. I suggested that she could trace her path around the island with her finger, telling the story as she went. This was quite successful, and I felt keen to find out if she would tolerate members of her family appearing on her island. I asked her if this would be OK – again, she was reluctant. That particular session ended, and I was satisfied that this kind of story work was not going to lead to any major breakthrough.

When Ellie arrived for therapy the following week, she had brought a case with her. Inside the case was a papier-mâché island – Ellie told me that she had thought about the work we had done, and that neither the imaginary island nor the drawn island felt 'solid' enough to have anyone else present. She had decided that she needed to create an island that had some substance to it. She had created several small characters and placed them in strategic locations on the island. This enabled her to begin recounting a story that allowed her to process many of the relationship problems she was encountering.

There were further developments to the story over subsequent sessions, which are not recalled here. I simply present this part of the case history as an example of how a multiple creative approach to story-making can enable the integration of at least some of the difficult feelings experienced by spectrum clients.

Chapter 10

Anger

Expressions of anger can create difficulties for individuals, especially where the expression is explosive in nature. This energy is directed outward, towards people or objects in the environment. It can involve verbal and physical aggression, and/or destructive behaviour. Other people in the environment will often experience negative emotional reactions to the anger. Some might respond with anger of their own or they might become fearful. There is a risk that the anger expressed by the person with autism will become viewed simply as a behaviour to be 'managed', rather than as an emotional expression which needs to be listened to. And where there is a behavioural focus, individuals often find themselves prescribed with various anti-psychotic medications and/or referred for 'anger management' support. This can mean that the original anger is never resolved. An essential task early in psychotherapeutic intervention around anger is, where possible, to identify and acknowledge the source of the distress. This can help to validate the spectrum client's feelings, and help to reduce sensitivities where appropriate.

Another type of expression is 'implosive' anger. Here, the anger is directed and contained inwardly, therefore making it far less noticeable. It can sit inside an individual's system, in some cases building up to a volcanic reservoir which eventually explodes, surprising everyone within the environment. In other cases, it becomes the fuel for negative states such as depression, certain types of self-harm and alcohol or drug dependence. Implosive anger is common where individuals are afraid of expressing their feelings, perhaps being anxious about the consequences of doing so. Intervention in these cases will often have at least part of its focus on increasing self-confidence and coaching assertiveness skills.

NICE Guidelines

In the UK, the National Institute for Health and Clinical Excellence (NICE) published its guidelines for the management of autism in adults in June 2012.[80] It made recommendations for anger management intervention as follows:

- functional analysis

- coping skills training and behaviour reversal

- relaxation training

- devclopment of problem-solving skills.

Functional analysis enables attempts to be made to discover the underlying reasons for a particular piece of behaviour. Patterns will often be discovered in either the antecedents (what led up to the behaviour) or consequences (what were the outcomes of the behaviour). Such analysis carries the risk of becoming a somewhat clinical exercise where the information gained usefully contributes to behaviour management, but fails to acknowledge the underlying emotional roots. A potential consequence of this might be that the target behaviour is reduced, but the emotional expression merely changes from being explosive to implosive. If the analysis recognises the anger behind particular behaviours, interventions can be planned that provide for better (and more useful) expression. Reflective analysis can enable those around the spectrum client to assess their own contribution, where appropriate, to that individual's emotional wellbeing.

Good functional analysis will lead to the identification of opportunities for coaching better coping skills. It will also provide scope for reversing particular behaviour patterns. Some individuals with autism spectrum conditions develop a default negative reactive behaviour pattern. Executive function difficulties for these individuals can lead to problems in generating alternative patterns of behaviour. The increased emotional arousal that often surrounds anger will further interfere with otherwise rational thought processes. Coaching can provide spectrum clients with these much-needed alternative strategies. For example, breathing techniques can be introduced for use when individuals become aware of their emotional temperature rising. Or they could be encouraged to remove themselves from the anger-provoking situation. This latter tactic might be difficult for a child in a classroom environment unless it is part of a strategy agreed upon by the class teacher and the school management team. The coaching of coping skills and behavioural alternatives need to form part of an overall intervention package that does not simply divert anger elsewhere. Positive and useful expression of anger is an essential element in maintaining emotional balance, and for some clients, support towards working at a resolution will be as helpful as coping and management skills.

Relaxation issues were discussed in Chapter 3. It is generally true that for people in emotional equilibrium, tolerance of certain negative experiences is increased. Tolerance is decreased if individuals feel stressed. Some people with autism spectrum conditions are described as having 'hair-trigger' reactions to relatively minor inconveniences or upsets. This may be reflective of the relative stress levels that individuals are experiencing, not least because they are having to navigate a social world that is not designed for them. Therapeutic intervention can be focused on bridging this gap, but in the meantime, there is also great value in teaching relaxation skills to spectrum clients (and in the provision of opportunities for relaxation, especially where there is a reduced intellectual capacity preventing the learning of new skills).

The development of problem-solving skills can help enormously in reducing frustration and anger. Cognitive Behavioural Therapy, coaching and story work are examples of interventions that will support such development. People on the autism spectrum sometimes have difficulty with generating alternative concepts. They can also find it problematic stringing together a cohesive understanding of cause and effect. Problem solving requires both these skills. Visual aids, such as charts, diagrams, storyboards, etc., will be useful in assisting spectrum clients to acquire such knowledge.

Cognitive Behavioural Therapy

Cognitive Behavioural Therapy is frequently recommended as the treatment of choice for anger management work – a situation that is supported by plenty of research evidence, as observed by Paxton and Estay (2007).[81] It is widely accepted that autism-friendly CBT can help clients, especially those with Asperger Syndrome, to develop better emotional regulation, and to replace distorted conceptualisations and dysfunctional beliefs. This can be achieved through the use of charting (see Chapter 5), and Social Stories™ (see Chapter 4). Tony Attwood (2004) provides additional suggestions around the provision of workbooks and the introduction of concepts such as a 'toolbox' to enable the development of a more robust problem-solving approach.[82] Workbooks enable people with Asperger Syndrome to follow a specific anger-management curriculum, whilst keeping and reviewing their own notes. The toolbox idea is the literal provision of ideas and suggestions of 'tools' to help manage situations better. The tools are a mixture of quick- and slow-release strategies, which are based around the practitioner's knowledge of the child and his or her situations. Tools may be categorised as 'physical' tools (activities for using up energy), 'relaxation' tools (activities that are calming), 'social' tools (identifying people to be with who can help), 'thinking' tools (introducing positive self-talk, for example, or establishing time for rational thought before reacting), and 'special interest tools' (using the person's interests and preferences to help restore equilibrium).

An essential element behind the success of a CBT approach lies in the provision of visual supports to help individuals identify their varying emotional states. Charting can provide this information. I have found that the actual chart used, and the information it conveys, will vary from individual to individual. Some will benefit from a simple tick chart; others might need the support of pictures and diagrams. Attwood (2004, p.4) presented the idea of emotional 'thermometers', where children with Asperger Syndrome are encouraged to draw a thermometer for a particular emotion.[83] Discussion around intensity leads to the placing of labels, or pictures, at various points on the thermometer. At the very least, children are enabled to recognise early warning signals of increasing emotional arousal, and can then be taught appropriate methods of communicating this to significant people in the environment (before the point of no return is reached).

Neuro-Linguistic Programming

Bill Goodyear (2008, pp.154–157) offers an extension of some of these CBT-based ideas from the perspective of coaching (and NLP).[84] He reminds us that for an adult, at least, anger management is very much a matter of choice. Clients' progress is usually more positive where they have consciously elected to engage with anger support. Goodyear asks, 'Can I change how I feel?' and 'Can I change what I do?' The coach, or therapist, will need to help the client answer these questions by pointing out possible alternatives. I have found that many adult clients have developed a negative pattern of responsive behaviour over many years, and for some, an explosive emotional response becomes a default reaction to things going wrong. They can see no alternative – unless one is presented to them. Behaviour management counselling that is limited to, 'Don't do that…' rarely achieves anything more than reinforcing the behaviour, because many people on the autism spectrum are unable to generate internal alternatives. I often use flowchart diagrams to show cause and effect of certain behavioural patterns, with similar diagrams to identify what might happen with alternative courses of action. This helps to attach essential value to managing anger – as discussed in Chapter 5, value is an important element in motivation.

Goodyear (2008, p.156) also reminds us of the difference between existential and specific anger. The former is perhaps best understood in terms of someone simply being generally angry. The latter is where someone might be cross because someone has used up all the milk again! Specific anger is probably more easily changed – in the case of the milk, it might be suggested that they take responsibility for keeping milk stocks up to date. Existential anger may prove to be more difficult to change, but improvements are certainly possible, especially if the individual is willing to accept some responsibility for the change, and is supported by his or her network. I have found that specific anger is best managed with a focused, problem-solving approach ('What can we do about this?'), whilst existential anger benefits from time-line or life story work (perhaps using the storyboard approach outlined in Chapter 9).

Mindfulness

Clients who play the 'blame game' often have difficulty with taking responsibility for their own emotional states. This happens because the individual becomes 'stuck' with their anger – it becomes attached to, or identified with, the situation, or other people, and is responded to with more anger being directed at it. A negative situation becomes even more negative, and this affects everybody within the environment. Other people react with further negativity – fear, anxiety or anger of their own. The conflicts thus created are rarely resolved. This can leave the client with a reservoir of impotent rage.

Where clients show an aptitude for focused attention, it is possible to teach an alternative 'mindful' approach. Whilst there is a need to acknowledge sources of distress, and to validate the feeling of anger, 'mindfulness' can steer an individual away from blaming other people, towards taking some responsibility for managing oneself. The approach involves coaching clients in being able to recognise and acknowledge their changing emotional states, before focusing their attention on directing positive and caring thoughts towards them. This can, where successful, prevent the negative cycle which starts with the explosive outward expression.

Assertiveness Coaching

For some spectrum clients, coaching in the art of assertiveness can be a useful way of directing and targeting anger more positively. I often describe this to clients as another way of avoiding the negative cycle of explosive energy, which often achieves nothing more than an inner resentment and rage. Rather, it is a way of using a precise laser beam to accurately and effectively focus anger in a useful direction. In some cases, it is simply a matter of discussing key statements to be delivered to relevant people. In others, work on self-esteem will need to be carried out first, enabling spectrum clients to be aware of their rights to good services, and environments where unreasonable demands and expectations are not continually being made.

I have worked with spectrum clients who can be described as 'passive'. Third-party referrers often state things like, 'We can't understand his recent outbursts. He likes everything we do for him.' In these cases, they may be living with, or working with, a person building a reservoir of anger, created by an inability to express dissatisfaction, or difficulty in saying 'No'. The client may have given up saying 'No' many years ago, having been placed in situations that dealt with such expressions as if they were challenging behaviour, which was thus 'managed' accordingly. Enabling such clients to reasonably say 'No' when appropriate (or, failing this, ensuring advocacy is available) can make a huge difference to behavioural expression.

Conflict Resolution

Conflict resolution can form an important part of dealing with anger on and around the autism spectrum. Avoidance of conflict in the first place might be an obvious suggestion, but this presumes that all the individuals involved in a situation have the benefit of typical executive functioning, and can therefore engage in forward planning (by no means guaranteed for those on the autism spectrum). It also presumes that all parties are *willing* to avoid conflict. Life will inevitably throw up situations in which there is a potential for disagreement, and practitioners can usefully support some spectrum clients with advice about how to deal effectively with these occurrences. There will also be a role for providing advice and support to those around the person with autism. For example, some families and agencies become bogged down by reaction and counter-reaction. In some cases individuals in the environment report that they have to 'tread on egg-shells', being fearful of an angry outburst in certain trigger situations.

My own approach is to take a 'no conflict – no problem' attitude, where at all possible. Whilst there are clear situations when an issue has to be confronted, perhaps for health and safety reasons, I have noticed that many of the conflict zones reported, concern battles that simply do not need to be fought. These can be described as 'Brussels sprout' moments – many adults may be able to identify with childhood situations in which they refused to eat certain foods, perhaps for reasons of taste, texture and/or smell. For me, it was Brussels sprouts, and the more my parents insisted that I eat them, the less likely I was to do so. We were in a conflict situation – within which the phrase, 'Eat them, they're good for you' was often heard. In fact, the conflict probably had more to do with power and control than a balanced diet (I ate everything else that was put in front of me). And it is often this quest for power and control that can create many of the battlegrounds around the autism spectrum.

An example of a common conflict zone for some spectrum clients surrounds personal hygiene. For those who do not wash often, anger erupts at the point of insistence from others, and for many this can come two or three times a day. Much of the conflict could be avoided by assessing whether the individual actually possesses the relevant sequencing skills required for bathing or showering – a simple task-focused sequencing aid could be valuable in such situations. If the individual possesses the skills, then advice might be targeted at removing the conflict entirely (i.e. getting people to stop nagging). This then creates the space for negotiation and/or coaching (especially if the person with autism desires more social contact).

This broadly fits Greene and Ablon's (2006) concept of using the Collaborative Problem Solving Approach[85] to reduce conflict. This involves Plan A, Plan B and Plan C. Plan A relates to the normal response to the conflict situation. A carer might become more insistent, with the result that the child or adult client becomes more entrenched, and may display an explosive reaction. Plan C refers to the removal of the conflict by simply dropping the insistence – in other words, the carer accepts the refusal. This enables the development of Plan B, to be implemented when things are calm. Plan B involves a collaborative, negotiated compromise, and the teaching of any absent skills.

Chapter 11

Anxiety

One of the major causes of difficult moments in autism is anxiety. Whilst anxiety can be described as a typical reaction to a stressor, prompting an individual to cope with a demanding situation, it can tip over into a state of high arousal and uneasiness. Physical symptoms can include fatigue, restlessness, muscle tension, nausea and pain. Acute anxiety can induce panic attacks, with associated hyper-ventilation. In autism, anxiety or panic can lead to the presentation of behavioural difficulties, withdrawal and isolation, and avoidance behaviour. Social situations, or sensory integration problems, are significant areas for experiencing anxiety on the autism spectrum.

Anxiety has its roots in the unknown, and as Sylvers, Lilienfeld and LaPrairie (2011) point out, much of it is anticipatory.[86] If a person is approaching a situation that they are unsure about, they are likely to be anxious. This can be because individuals do not know what is expected of them, or do not know what is about to happen. Such states can be regular occurrences for people with autism, especially if their perceptions and perspectives on life are atypical. The use of obsessional interests and ritualistic behaviours can be useful defence mechanisms employed by people with autism when experiencing anxiety. They can in fact be a useful barometer in assessing stress levels – an increase in such behaviours can indicate raised anxiety, and a drop can mean the individual is approaching better equilibrium. Where such coping strategies and defence mechanisms interfere with daily living, or do not enable the person to cope, support will be needed. Relaxation techniques, thought stoppers and pharmaceutical interventions were identified in Chapter 3. It will be useful to consider additional strategies in more detail.

Cognitive Behavioural Therapy

An excellent cognitive behavioural resource is The Incredible 5-Point Scale, created by Kari Dunn Buron and Mitzi Curtis (2003).[87] Although predominantly aimed at children with autism spectrum conditions, the system is easily adaptable for adults. The resource is not simply applicable to anxiety – it can also be used to help with anger, obsessions and social proximity. Essentially, the practitioner and the person with autism work together to devise a scale from 1 to 5 (1 being the optimum situation, and 5 being the worst case scenario). In the case of anxiety, having no worries is scored as 1, and being out of control is scored as 5. Descriptions of the various scenarios are identified, as well as the behavioural reactions. The scales are then used to assist individuals to self-regulate their reactivity, leading to an ability to calm themselves down. Self-awareness and self-regulation can lead to opportunities for spectrum clients to develop alternative strategies. The calming strategies that are employed need to be easily available to avoid creating further anxiety whilst looking for them.

Further cognitive behavioural support can be offered in the form of desensitisation in the case of specific anxiety, particularly phobic reactions. An example might be the overwhelming fear of dogs. If on assessment it is decided that there is no sensory element involved, the spectrum client can be encouraged to give an example of a dog that would be considered 'safe'. This could be a dog far away on the horizon, or one that is very well trained. A scale could be drawn up (perhaps a five-point scale!) with the idea of gradually encouraging the consideration of closer proximity, at least until the anxiety has reached more natural levels.

It is sometimes useful to assist clients to recognise the difference between irrational and functional anxiety. A functional anxiety is actually quite useful – it is a way of being aware of danger. It stops us walking too near the edge of a cliff, or creates the motivation to move if we smell smoke at the same time as hearing a fire alarm. An irrational fear or anxiety can merely interfere with normal daily functioning. Some spectrum clients benefit from being part of a process to construct two lists (preferably on the same page) – one identifying functional anxieties, the other specifying examples of irrational fears. It can be useful to clarify the actual risk of harm in each case. This kind of approach is sometimes referred to as cognitive restructuring – replacing cognitive distortions with more rational thoughts. Paxton and Estay (2007) use a metaphor describing cognitive distortions as 'thought poisons', with rational responses being the 'antidotes'.[88]

Cresswell and Willetts (2007) offer additional advice around CBT and anxiety in children.[89] Whilst not specifically aimed at children on the autism spectrum, their insights can easily be used with spectrum clients. In their section 'Is That a Helpful Thought' (pp.62–72) they encourage the evaluation of anxious thoughts, and accentuate the benefits of getting the child to think things through rationally, keeping thought records and testing the fears. For example, they suggest that, for a fear of looking stupid in class if the child were to give a wrong answer, the child be given the task of noting when other children get an answer wrong and recording the response.

Programming and Information to Reduce Anxiety

If it is accepted that at least some anxiety has its roots in 'not knowing', then the provision of information can provide people with a sense of greater control. Information equals knowledge, and with apologies to Sir Francis Bacon, knowledge is power. Effective timetabling, Social Stories™, charts, scripts, etc., can all help to ease anxiety about forthcoming situations.

Other useful information can be provided in the form of emergency procedures. These can be written into programmes and Social Stories™. It is helpful for people with autism spectrum conditions to have access to emergency telephone numbers, and scripts to use in particular situations. One client was referred to me by his employer's occupational health staff because he would not take his scheduled breaks. He worked for a national retail company and, on investigation, it appeared that he could not deal with the chaotic nature of the staff canteen at the store where he worked. I asked him why he did not go out for his breaks. He replied, 'Because there are people out there.' I observed that there were people in the store, and he responded by saying, 'Yes, but I know what they're here for – they're doing their shopping. I have no idea what the people out in the street are doing. I'm afraid someone might talk to me.' I asked him what he thought they might say. He considered for a moment, and answered, 'They might ask me for directions, and I might not know the way. And I can't predict whether I will know or not before they've asked. What should I do?' We discussed the relative value of several potential responses, and he eventually decided upon a standard, 'I'm sorry, I can't help, I don't know the way' – even if he knew. He was particularly enamoured of the concept of being able to get away with a 'little white lie'.

Inveterate spectrum worriers may be operating a system that *needs* anxiety. I have worked with clients for whom if there is nothing to worry about, they will invent something. This can be more of a problem for those around the individual than for the client him- or herself. In some cases, we have been able to institute 'worry time' into their routine or schedule. This provides for specific times and locations where worries can be discussed. The client is encouraged to write new anxieties down to bring to the scheduled 'worry time'. For other constant worriers, their repeated searching for reassurance may point to a need to receive information in a specific way. Visually supported answers will be useful for visual processors, whilst digital recordings can help those who need to 'hear' information repeated. Clients can be directed to these tangible reminder systems at times of increased anxiety.

Hypnotherapy

Chapter 8 described in detail the value of hypnotherapy for work across the autism spectrum. In particular, dialogue work, anchoring, the control room and SWISH techniques can be of use around anxiety. These techniques can either reduce anxiety in themselves, or contribute to greater confidence about forthcoming situations. Hypnosis can also help in cases of Generalised Anxiety Disorder – clients can present with constant symptoms of anxious arousal, where the anxiety is irrational and disproportionate to the actual situation. Teaching self-hypnotic techniques will be most useful in these cases, as it enables clients to continue the work outside of the therapy room. As Heather (2011) points out, sufficient practice enables the replacement of the 'anxious' habit with the new habit of being calm.[90]

For some clients, the cautious use of regression work can identify root causes of anxiety issues. Therapists need to be sensitive to the risk of exposing spectrum clients to further trauma and anxiety, especially if they are already ruminative or catastrophic thinkers. Some clients already remember traumatic experiences exactly as they happened (this is called revivification), and regression work might be contra-indicated here. Where there are no such risks (or the therapist is skilled enough to suggest instant exit strategies), deep-rooted specific anxieties can be investigated. With one client (referred for hypnosis for dog phobia), discussion revealed that revivification was unlikely. The client was unable to explain the phobia, and confirmed that he had never been bitten, was very rarely barked at, and had had the fear for as long as he could remember. On regression, he described being two and a half years old, and was playing on his hands and knees with a Jack Russell terrier belonging to his uncle. The dog had never been aggressive towards a human. The client remembered clearly being face to face with the dog, enjoying being licked. His mother entered the room, and on seeing the pair on the floor immediately assumed that the dog was attacking her son. It was actually her scream that completely terrified the child – my client was able to identify with the displacement of the fear of his mother's reaction onto dogs. This is not to suggest that other clients with a fear of dogs have the same experience as a root cause – many spectrum clients report difficulties with sound sensitivities, for example, and find the unpredictable barking of a dog to be a problem. I merely present this case as an example that people on the autism spectrum can experience similar emotional consequences as the general population.

Social Anxiety

Social anxiety is a phenomenon that can be experienced both on and off the autism spectrum. Neurotypical people often report nervousness around job interviews, for example. They might experience shyness, especially around 'authority' figures, and may avoid public speaking opportunities. These issues do not often interfere with general life functioning. For many people on the autism spectrum, however, social anxiety can present a major challenge. The anxiety around social situations stems from poor social competence. This is due to the problems with the essential 'connections' so usefully made by more neuro- or socially-typical people. It means that people on the spectrum may not get the practice, or feedback, from interactions that can then go on to inform future social behaviour. Conflict can follow, and thus socialising can become intimidating. Clients can become hyper-vigilant or paranoid about other people's reactions to them, and can become hyper-sensitive to criticism. This is particularly true of the proportion of the spectrum population with Asperger Syndrome, many of whom report for therapeutic support with feelings of isolation, loneliness and depression. Social coaching, combined with cognitive restructuring, can provide a powerful antidote to this negativity and anxiety. Confidence can be built using planning and preparation techniques, and these can be enhanced with hypnosis and/or goal and target setting. Social Stories™ can help to fill in some of the gaps in social awareness.

Some practitioners find themselves working with individuals on the spectrum who may be completely socially avoidant. This can be due to extreme withdrawal – for example, clients may have experienced such negativity within attempts at interaction that they have literally given up. I worked with one man who had refused to leave his bedroom for four months, following a succession of negative incidents at college (most involving female peers). He regarded all attempts to get him to leave his room as hostile. Our first few sessions consisted of home visits. He refused to see me on the first occasion – in fact, he told me emphatically through his closed (and locked) bedroom door to 'Go away!' Rather than attempt to argue with him (conflict), or to persuade him to let me in, I felt it appropriate to respect his isolation. I returned the following week, to receive the same greeting as before. This time I simply sat at the top of the stairs in the house he shared with his family. He unlocked his door, stuck his head out, and said, 'I thought I told you to go away!' I saw this as progress (from two words behind a door to a whole sentence with eye contact), and told his family I would return the next week. Not only did he unlock his door again, but he invited me inside. We made some good progress, and it was not long before he was coming to my therapy rooms for sessions. When I asked him why he had let me in to his room, he simply said, 'Because you were the first person not to try and get me to come out.' Part of our work together comprised rebuilding his shattered confidence in small steps, factoring in, as Tony Attwood (1998, p.155) describes them, specific islands of solitude.[91] These are simply allocated times during a day, or week, for clients to be 'left alone', enabling them to recover somewhat from the often exhausting task that is social contact.

Other clients' social avoidance may be a result of being completely self-absorbed, or locked within the sensory feedback loops provided by their own systems. If it is felt that attempts need to be made to encourage social development, then approaches such as Intensive Interaction (see Chapter 6) will be useful.

NICE Guidelines

The National Institute for Health and Clinical Excellence published guidelines (2012) for the management of autism in the UK. These have already been mentioned in Chapter 10, where recommendations were made for anger management on the autism spectrum. The same document (p.39) suggested that there was a need for research around the clinical and cost effectiveness of facilitated self-help for the treatment of mild anxiety and depressive disorders in adults with autism.[92] The report cites that, traditionally, there has been low take-up of potential beneficial services due to poor access and availability, and also because such services have not been adapted for use with this population. Some of the integrative psychotherapeutic measures mentioned in this book may go some way towards providing such services.

Obsessional Compulsive Disorder

This condition can be co-morbid with autism spectrum disorder, and is characterised by repetitive, obsessional thoughts, usually alongside a compulsive drive to perform particular actions or rituals. Such actions can include a range of activities, such as repeated hand-washing, door-closing, light-switching and prevaricating on thresholds. Obsessional Compulsive Disorder (OCD) is often stress-reactive, and a major stress in the lives of many spectrum clients is anxiety. When considering the potential presence of OCD in autism, it should be remembered that at least some of the repetitive and ritualistic behaviours seen on the autism spectrum are simple coping mechanisms and function as self-calming activities. Caution should be exercised when considering the removal of these behaviours – the risk is that the client will be exposed to unmitigated stress without a coping mechanism. If the behaviours are not thought to be inappropriate, and do not interfere with daily living, then intervention is not necessary. Some of the behaviours may need channelling into more appropriate times and locations (timetabling can work well here). Where the behaviours do interfere with safe daily living, then intervention of some sort is warranted.

Pharmacological interventions are sometimes used in the treatment of OCD, within both the typical and autistic populations. Paxton and Estay (2007, p.133) note that pharmaceutical approaches for OCD benefit between 40 and 60 per cent of the general population, whose symptoms are improved by 20 to 40 per cent.[93] Effectively, this means that maybe half the symptoms of OCD can be treated in about half the general population, using drugs such as selective serotonin reuptake inhibitors (SSRIs). It is clear that additional approaches will need to be considered. CBT techniques will be useful here – for example, frequency charts can help individuals to notice when they have carried out a particular action, and this can prevent the need to repeat the action. The hypnotherapeutic control room technique is another example of a suitable intervention – clients can be helped to 'turn down' the compulsion controls to a more acceptable level.

Chapter 12

Loss and Bereavement

As noted in Chapter 2, we are beginning to explode some of the myths involving learning disability and autism spectrum conditions around bereavement. The death of a significant person rarely goes unnoticed, even if the expression of grief is unusual, or appears non-existent. And even when a client is able to express grief, he or she can become 'stuck' in one of the various stages. For example, an adult client from a Jewish background adhered to a strict year-long mourning period following the death of her father, avoiding television, the radio, parties, social gatherings, etc. This mourning ritual became a way of life and she found it really difficult to re-engage with the activities she had enjoyed prior to the loss. She became deeply depressed and fixated on her father's absence. Part of her solution involved straightforward coaching in the stages of bereavement, and the creation of a memorial display to enable the externalisation and diffusion of her difficult-to-manage internal feelings. These topics are discussed in more detail below.

For some people on the autism spectrum, the experience of loss occurs far more frequently than in the neurotypical population, and may be connected to things other than significant friends and family. I have worked with clients who worked through grief at every transition – they were so focused on the task in hand that it was a major wrench to have to move on. Others display grief when required to give up an object to which they have become attached. For example, an adult male client was devastated at the thought of having to give up carrying his teddy bear around when shopping – his carers were concerned that he was being bullied by local youths. Part of his solution involved a story-making approach – we created a story in which the bear was crowned 'King' of the hallway behind the client's front door. The bear was a very good king, and liked to stay behind to look after the kingdom when the client went out. This proved to be effective, and was the starting point for his carers to be able to create a strategy to develop a more age-appropriate perspective.

These observations make it clear that individuals on the autism spectrum experience grief in very personal and perhaps idiosyncratic ways. Hence the value of 'autism-aware' counsellors being able to guide spectrum clients through their own individual bereavement pathway. Rachel Forrester-Jones and Sarah Broadhurst (2008) provide an excellent range of advice for supporting people with autism through grief and bereavement in their book *Autism and Loss*.[94] They confirm that grief can be experienced not solely around death, but also around the loss of social relationships, home and possessions, role and identity, and health and wellbeing. Examples of circumstances that may impact on each of these additional areas include the need to change schools, the passage from school to adulthood, and, for some, admission into residential placements. Where a person with autism has care needs that prevent independent living, the death of either or both parents will often result in dealing with loss in all of the areas listed. For others, divorcing parents can lead to a significant change in circumstances.

Preparation and Explanation

The fact that death is one of the secrets kept from people with a learning disability was mentioned in Chapter 2.

Our reluctance to address these issues means that often we only discuss bereavement when it is too late. Two of the best ways of enabling individuals to deal with loss and bereavement are preparation and explanation. A third is acknowledging that grief is a normal and natural process in life, and denying someone the opportunity to grieve can have very serious consequences, both emotionally and behaviourally. It is widely accepted that, in general, people with autism spectrum conditions thrive on clarity and the absence of surprises – the benefits of good planning strategies apply to bereavement as much as to any of the other areas discussed previously. Such planning can help individuals and those supporting them to prepare for, and work through, their grief – together.

Social Stories™, timetables and calendars can all be used to help people with autism prepare for forthcoming change. Whilst it may seem callous, these aids can also be used to identify an approaching death. An additional use of Social Stories™ will be helping to explain things like terminal illness, or why relatives have to visit hospital. Discussing such events logically in everyday language enables everyone involved, not just the person with autism, to anticipate a death. Using examples of the passing of distant relatives and pets can help to normalise death, and whilst it will not remove the pain of a significant and/or sudden death when it happens, it does remove much of the anxiety that stems from not knowing what is happening. People with autism can be involved in observing some of the funeral rituals surrounding death within their particular culture, well in advance of having to do it for a family member. When explaining the process of death to a spectrum client, it is useful to bear in mind the potential for concrete interpretations of euphemisms. For example, the sentence, 'Granny has gone to sleep' might lead to an expectation that we will see Granny in the morning. And whilst the concept of heaven, etc., is understood by some people on the spectrum, it might too abstract for others (whatever the belief system of those supporting them). Allison (2001) suggests explaining death in the context of a life cycle, using insects, plants or animals.[95] This practical approach is logical, clear and can be presented visually.

Working Through Loss

Some people with autism, especially those who think in particularly concrete terms, seem to be able to deal with the loss of a significant person in a purely matter-of-fact way, at least on the surface. This apparent lack of regard may be reflective of a true state of disconnectedness from the deceased once they have gone. However, it may also reflect an inability to express (or deal with) underlying emotion. Significant behavioural changes or manifestations of depression, anger or anxiety can follow – sometimes several months after the death. In these cases, and, of course, in cases where spectrum clients show more obvious signs of grief issues, practitioners need to offer support to enable effective transition to life without the deceased.

J. William Worden (1991, pp.10–18) offers a useful model of four tasks that are involved in working through grief.[96] The tasks are:

1. to accept that the loss is real

2. to work through the pain of the grief

3. to adjust to life without the deceased

4. to relocate the deceased emotionally, allowing energy to be transferred from the grief to something new, i.e. moving on.

This model lends itself to working with people on the autism spectrum because it provides a clear process, and allows for goal and target setting. It acknowledges that there will be emotional pain within the process. We have seen previously that emotional content which proves difficult to hold internally can be externalised through the use of story-making, drawing, and using dolls or puppets, etc. Where the spectrum client was dependent upon the deceased person, then there may be real difficulties in adjustment. This will be especially true where there was a lack of preparation. It will be necessary to carry out ego-strengthening (or self-esteem) work, and this can involve setting tasks and goals, and addressing (by assessment) outstanding dependency issues.

Saying 'Goodbye'

Enabling the client to participate in a funeral ritual in some way helps to establish the finality of the relationship. For some, attendance at the main funeral service and burial/cremation will be possible. Others, however, may find the social situation to be too distressing in itself, and support here could be offered by way of enabling participation with a small group of relatives before or after the main gathering, or perhaps even having their own private ritual. I sometimes explain to clients that before we can say 'Hello' to the 'new', we need to say 'Goodbye' to the 'old'. Nearly every culture within mankind has developed essential funeral rituals – it is almost as if we have a deep need of being able to mark the passing of those we love. It is worth remembering that the client is likely to have an emotional reaction within the funeral ritual – this is entirely normal and natural, even if the reaction itself is atypical, i.e. giggling instead of crying. For some families and carers, there is anxiety around these emotional reactions, and this is often a reason cited for not encouraging attendance at the funeral ('He will find it too distressing'). It can be useful to sensitively remind those families and carers that such shared expression is part of the point of such rituals – an opportunity for collective leave-taking. Denying attendance makes it very difficult for the individual to reach a resolution, which makes it very hard to move on.

Memorial

At the same time as acknowledging the passing of the deceased, it is also important to provide opportunities for remembrance and memorial. The presence of the deceased before death contributes to the life story of those who survive. Where appropriate, there is scope for practitioners to work with spectrum clients around building up a reminiscence system, perhaps by creating a memorial book, using information and photographs from the deceased's life. People with autism may not be naturally experienced at reminiscence. Atypical executive function can mean that some find it difficult to develop a cohesive and balanced 'connection' between concepts and different experiences. There is a risk that individual pieces of experience will be focused on in ruminative or perseverative ways, contributing to anger or depression. Hence the value of work to construct a good reminiscence process, enabling more balanced perspectives of an individual's overall story.

Alternative memorial devices might revolve around the planting of a tree, or shrub, in the deceased's memory, or the creation of a whole memorial garden. I am aware of a therapist who encouraged a spectrum client to create a small 'shrine' in her bedroom, in keeping with the client's stated preference of religious observance. The shrine was a simple photograph in a frame, with candles that could be lit when necessary. The client was enabled to redirect negative emotional energy away from the rest of her environment into a simple daily act of remembrance. Memorial processes can also help in compensating the experience of those spectrum clients unable to attend the main funeral service.

Looking Ahead

An awareness of our own story, and of those who have contributed to it, is an essential element of knowing who we are. This, in turn, enables us to consider where we are headed.

The leave-taking and the memorial process can be seen as waypoints along the journey into the future. Bereaved people on the autism spectrum may need to be assisted to turn their attention to life without the deceased. For some it might be necessary to identify how their new social network looks, and which part of it can be used to replace the function or value of the person who has died. This same kind of work might also need to be applied in the case of spectrum clients who react badly to things like staff turnover.

Chapter 13

Positive Life Planning

This chapter probably has more to do with coaching than any of the others. Good planning can help spectrum clients to avoid many of the pitfalls which may have littered their paths so far. These pitfalls will have caused or contributed to the emotional reactions that preceded the referral for therapeutic support. It is incumbent upon therapists and counsellors to ensure that following a return to emotional wellbeing, spectrum clients have opportunities for engagement with an effective planning process. Those counselling practitioners who have received training in coaching may be best placed to continue working with the relevant clients. Others might need to refer to an experienced, autism-aware coach. There can be professional boundary issues for practitioners moving from a counselling relationship with a client to one that involves coaching. This should not be a problem for integrative therapists, particularly those supported by a robust supervision arrangement. However it is done, the transition from counselling to coaching can play an important part in reducing the risk of the revolving-door experience of therapeutic intervention, where clients complete a course of therapy only to return a few months later because they have somehow arrived at the same negative place in their lives that triggered the first referral. It is almost as if coaching, or support for effective planning, needs to be considered a compulsory final part of the counselling process for spectrum clients.

Barriers to Self-determination

The ability to positively plan, if not for the whole of life, at least for segments of it, is an important part of self-determination – the ability to be in control of our lives, making positive choices without hindrance or interference from others. If people feel that their lives are controlled by others, it can have a detrimental effect on psychological and emotional wellbeing. There are implicit barriers to self-determination arising from an autism spectrum condition. Executive functioning difficulties can mean that the actual process of planning is difficult. Some people with autism live very much in the 'here and the now', which means that engaging with the past (evaluation) or with the future (planning) is almost impossible without support and advice. A concrete thinking style may hinder an imaginative thought process, particularly if the 'future' is seen as an abstract entity. Social anxiety may inhibit motivation to engage in thinking about work or leisure opportunities. And communication difficulties can mean that even where a spectrum clients have an idea of what they want to do, they are potentially unable to express it.

But there can also be further barriers beyond the autism itself. If clients have experienced a great deal of negativity, they can develop low self-esteem, depression and limiting beliefs. These are not good motivators for engaging with a positive future. Additionally, people around individuals can, either wittingly or unwittingly, work to prevent some spectrum clients reaching their full potential. For example, the spectrum individual may be seen as a vulnerable, disabled person, in need of protection rather than exposure to the 'big wide world'. Alternatively, there can be an assumption that the individual will 'never amount to much', and this can be unconsciously communicated and taken on board.

Practitioners thus need to be aware of these influences, and, where considered appropriate, to assist spectrum clients in gaining a balanced perspective on their story 'so far'. Storyboards and life story work will be of value here (see Chapter 9). Successful support for planning relies on an accurate assessment of current circumstances, informed by an understanding and evaluation of the past, before enabling engagement with the future.

Inevitably, some spectrum clients will find that their lives are subject to supervision and surveillance, due to their 'special needs'. To enhance the centrality of such people to their networks, it will be important to energise an effective communication process between families, advocates, agencies, funding departments and key workers. This will be of little value to the individual at the centre unless he or she is involved in the communicative process somehow. Sadly, reducing lifestyle planning for an individual to a succession of committee meetings (where some important members of that committee rarely meet the client) is not conducive to that client having any sense of control. Such an approach is unlikely to motivate clients to participate, even if they do attend. It is important to ensure that discussions do not simply take place 'around' the client. Therapists who become aware of such situations can support clients with assertiveness and/or refer for advocacy. There may also be scope for implementing relaxation techniques, social coaching and anger management strategies. It is tempting to become involved in the communication process, and in some cases this may be necessary, but it will be important to consider issues surrounding professional boundaries and confidentiality.

Person Centred Planning

An important tool that has become popular for work with supported clients is a process known as Person Centred Planning.

Bob Gates (2007, p.304) states that, 'Instead of trying to "fix" people, the focus of person-centred planning is to discover what an individual's chosen lifestyle is and how this can be achieved.'[97] Counsellors and therapists can become involved in this process by assisting clients to identify what it is they want from life and how this is to be achieved, and then to be able to communicate around their network. Many of the techniques described earlier in this book lend themselves to this kind of work – from straightforward talking about things, through life story work (projecting ahead), and creative approaches, etc.

Visual systems are common in Person Centred Planning. Social networks that identify key people in a person's life can be illustrated. MAPS (Making Action Plans) and PATHS (Planning Alternative Tomorrows with Hope)[98] can encourage clients to think about their life journeys, their goals and their aspirations. Each can be illustrated. There is a sense in which these processes mirror the cognitive behavioural work of setting goals and targets, identifying the various steps that need to be completed when moving towards the goal. Some spectrum clients struggle with the abstract concepts of dreams and aspirations. It may be necessary to use more concrete language (such as goals and targets) or to offer discussion or explanation of what dreams and aspirations might mean to individuals. We are essentially getting clients to identify with two key questions: 'What have you got?' and 'What do you want?' A useful supplementary question might be, 'What *don't* you want?'

Issues for Adulthood

Psychological and emotional harm can be experienced by spectrum clients during the transition period from adolescent to adult. The expectations of the adult world are very different to the expectations placed on a child in a child's world. One client told me, 'I just about had a handle on things during my school days. I couldn't have survived it without the support that I had. As I left school, I was told that I was an adult now – and they took all the support away.' Many therapists are faced with the task of unravelling the effects of this transitionary trauma – often clients cannot engage in a positive planning process until this is done.

I have worked with several clients who have come 'unstuck' as they have tried to cope with adult life. In some cases, it has been assumed that they have made appropriate decisions, without realising that capacity for making informed choices in those individuals is very small. In two cases referred for 'behavioural difficulties' or 'anger management', it became apparent that the clients were simply unhappy with their lifestyles, even though each had apparently made a choice to live in their domiciliary accommodation. Both were 'here and now' people, which meant they had difficulty evaluating (which requires an ability to look back) and planning (which requires an ability to look ahead). It also meant they had difficulty in comparing and contrasting different options. Both were asked questions like, 'Where do you want to live?' whilst physically present in the buildings they currently lived in. It is not surprising that their answer was along the lines of 'Here, please.' No-one had appreciated that they were unable to bring to mind images of the previous accommodation options they had been shown. What this means is that even where choices are expressed, a process of checking needs to be undertaken. When working with clients around accommodation and employment, for example, I will often use mind-mapping and listing techniques to elicit informed choices.

Transitional Support

Anxiety about transition can be assuaged by providing information. Letting people know what might be expected, or what is to happen, enables transitions to be smoother. Taster days, trial periods, photographs, video footage and testimonials are all examples of potential transitional assistance. Whilst it is to be hoped that those supporting clients generally are able to provide advance information, etc., spectrum clients navigating life without such support might need the help of their counsellor or coach in these situations. I tend to make sure I have access to the internet during counselling sessions, so that a quick and instant 'search' can be undertaken for relevant images, articles or explanations.

Independence vs Dependence

Encouraging and promoting independence are useful aims of any kind of support for spectrum clients. But it is hard to ignore the fact that the person being supported is, in effect, dependent on that support. This can be a tricky conundrum for counsellors trying to avoid clients becoming too dependent on them. And it can be a difficult problem for some clients too, as they desperately attempt to fulfil the expectation of independent living, regarding themselves as failures if they don't quite make it. Hollins' (2000) observation that dependency was one of the three 'secrets' kept from people with a learning disability[99] (sex and death were the other two) was mentioned in Chapter 2. Her contention is that a failure to honestly represent these concepts in the life of a person with a learning disability contributes to psychological and emotional difficulty (over and above that caused by having the disability itself).

I have found that, for some clients, just a simple acknowledgement of the fact that it is hard to reconcile these apparently opposing issues is enough. Others find charts and diagrams of the characteristics of the two useful. Where possible, I try to get clients to consult their 'internal dictionary', to provide information about how they see the differing concepts. It is then possible to carry out a 'reframe' exercise to provide a balanced perspective. Part of this involves suggestions from me about where the middle ground lies (I call it 'inter-dependence'). Whilst most neurotypical adults refer to themselves as independent, very few would consider life entirely without anyone else. This ties in with work on social networks – we are largely reliant on them, particularly for affirmation, respect, trust, guidance, etc. We can thus populate the middle ground with positive messages. This clears the way for discussion about things that we are not so good at, where we may need to rely on someone else in a practical sense. These 'lacks' can then more easily be acknowledged and placed within the planning process. There is clearly a knock-on effect in terms of self-esteem.

I have also found it useful on occasion to focus for a while on the skills and special interests that a client may have.

These discussions can lead into an exercise in comparing clients' views of their ideal self with their perceived self, with a view to identifying ways of bringing them closer together. If this proves to be a difficult concept for clients, I can ask them to list a small number of good points and bad points about themselves. I will then ask them to get trusted people to write down five good things about them, so that we can compare them at a following session. This at least enables clients to see themselves from someone else's point of view. For those spectrum clients with a past-focused orientation, or those who live simply in the 'here and the now', these 'positive' reframes will be essential in enabling them to engage with a Positive Life Planning process.

Chapter 14

New Developments

There are always advances being made in the application of therapeutic approaches with any client group. At the time of writing, two particular techniques are proving to be popular with practitioners and clients: Emotional Freedom Technique (EFT) and Eye Movement Desensitisation and Reprocessing (EMDR). Either can be used as a 'stand-alone' intervention, although they both lend themselves very well to integrative work alongside other approaches. Their description here is not intended to be a substitute for formal training in these methods – they are mentioned because, despite the absence of reliable research into their efficacy on the autism spectrum, anecdotal evidence is generally very positive.

Emotional Freedom Technique

EFT, first formulated in its current form by Gary Craig (2011), combines aspects of CBT and NLP with the use of acupressure points on the body. In this sense it can be said that EFT is an amalgam of elements of western psychological practice with eastern medical philosophy. In *The EFT Manual* (2011, p.55), Craig suggests that EFT dramatically reduces the number of therapeutic sessions required to register improvement, compared with straightforward CBT.[100] A client experiencing emotional distress is asked to score their distress on a Subjective Units of Distress (SUD) scale. This might involve remembering a traumatic incident, or picturing an argument with a significant person. Once a score is arrived at, the client is then asked to simultaneously recite an agreed sentence regarding the distress (followed by a self-affirming statement), whilst lightly tapping various acupressure points on the head and upper body. In essence, the client is participating in cognitive restructuring, or reframing a limiting belief, supported by an 'energy release' mechanism. At the end of the process, clients will be asked to re-score their emotional distress on the SUD scale.

The absence of scientific research into the use of EFT on the autism spectrum was mentioned above. There is, however, a growing body of research suggesting that EFT is beneficial towards the treatment of Post-Traumatic Stress Disorder (PTSD), phobias, anxiety, depression and pain. David Fenstein (2012) has provided a useful review of available research findings.[101] He describes how latest theories revolve around the action of stimulating acupressure points on the limbic system. In short, light tapping, or pressure, on an acupressure point seems to arrest the body's automatic arousal system that sends a fight or flight message during the act of remembering a traumatic incident or emotional experience. In this way, SUD scores can be dramatically reduced, following only a small number of sessions.

The amount of anecdotal evidence for the efficacy of EFT around the autism spectrum is growing (see, for example, Lewis 2007[102]). Part of its growing popularity is the ease of learning, enabling spectrum clients to self-administer the treatment, in similar fashion to learning relaxation techniques or self-hypnosis. This 'self-help' element is attractive to many clients because it gives a sense of control over the emotional content of life that can create so many problems. Some degree of scepticism has been reported regarding EFT, particularly around the fact that it is hard to distinguish between the technique and the 'placebo' effect.[103] This criticism can be levelled at many psychotherapeutic techniques. However, in essence, the point of any treatment, whether pharmacological, psychological or physiological, is the improvement or removal of symptoms – and both the practitioner and client/patient know this. Both will therefore emotionally 'subscribe' to the anticipation of a positive effect, and this potentially makes a positive result more likely. Many EFT practitioners point to the fact that their clients have already tried other approaches without success, and would thus suggest that there must be something active in the EFT that does not form part of the other systems. Whether this lies in the manipulation of 'energy' points on the body, or in the conscious application of positive psychology (or both!), remains to be seen.

Eye Movement Desensitisation and Reprocessing

EMDR is similar to EFT in that it adds an element of physiological stimulation to standard CBT models of treatment, particularly 'exposure therapy' (asking a client to actively re-engage with a traumatic incident by describing it in detail – this, of course, risks an abreaction, which spectrum clients can find as distressing as the original trauma) and cognitive restructuring (identifying and challenging limiting or maladaptive thinking). The physiological stimulation usually involves a guided series of eye movements, together with tapping on alternate sides of the body (sometimes replaced with finger clicking) and the use of bilateral sound tones. The 'exposure' element is greatly reduced – rather than relate the entire traumatic experience, clients are asked to focus on a particular element of it. As with EFT, EMDR is described as greatly reducing the number of therapeutic sessions required for an improvement in symptomology to be observed, compared with CBT. The approach was developed by Francine Shapiro during the late 1980s, and summarised in her book co-written with Margot Silk Forrest (1997).[104] The various bilateral stimulation processes that occur alongside mental imagery are said to promote the association of positive information processing (in other words, a restructuring of the traumatic memory).

Sceptics have questioned the need for the bilateral stimulation on top of already successful CBT techniques, especially as there has to date been little plausible explanation of how the eye movements, etc., are meant to work.[105] In the introduction to her book, Shapiro's response to criticisms such as this has been to posit that perhaps the stimulatory actions cause an 'orienting' or 'interest' response in the brain which speeds the reprocessing of disturbing memories, or that the eye movements in particular mirror the brain activity experienced during REM (Rapid Eye Movement) sleep.[106] It is interesting to note that the guided eye movements prevalent in EMDR are reminiscent of some of the early forms of hypnotic induction, which used a swinging pendulum or pocket watch to precede the trance-state or relaxation. This relaxed state enhances suggestibility to material either produced by the client or offered by the therapist. The field of hypnotherapy can offer an additional support to Shapiro's suggestion that the other physical stimuli (alternate body tapping and/or the use of bilateral auditory tones) arouse the brain's interest system – a hypnotherapist will sometimes deliberately use confusional techniques during hypnotic induction (particularly where the patient is focused on trauma) to give the conscious mind something else to focus on, allowing the sub-conscious mind to assist in reprocessing.

There is little research pointing to the efficacy of EMDR with autism spectrum conditions. However, recent attention is being paid to anecdotal evidence. Joanne Morris-Smith (2007) has suggested that there are aspects of the EMDR protocol that might make it suitable for use with some children with autism.[107] She noted that it seems to enable work with pre-verbal memory, and helps to link sensorily-stored memory with verbal expression to help in processing. Mevissen, Lievegoed and de Jongh (2011) present a case study of four people with intellectual disabilities and PTSD, one of whom was an 11-year-old boy with a diagnosis of autism spectrum disorder.[108] Five sessions of EMDR resulted in a complete removal of PTSD symptoms, a restoration of the client into his family home, and after six weeks his diagnosis of autism spectrum disorder no longer applied.

Historical Influences on Psychotherapy for Autism

A therapist or counsellor wishing to work more effectively with clients on the autism spectrum can do so without reading the following notes. However, as observed in Chapter 13 ('Positive Life Planning'), information about where we have come from can help to explain where we are, and the combination of these two perspectives can provide a useful platform for looking into the future. These notes are therefore provided as historical background for those who might be interested. They outline some of the important personalities and theories relevant to the development of therapeutic approaches to autism, the study of which has contributed to my own understanding and practice.

Leo Kanner (1894–1981)

Adam Feinstein (2010, p.7) points out that there is some debate as to which of Kanner and Asperger (see below) was the first to actually use the term 'autistic',[109] but it is Kanner's paper (1943) that set the scene for what is now regarded as describing childhood autism.[110] He was an Austrian child psychiatrist. In his paper, based on 11 children, referred to his clinic in the USA over a period of several years, Kanner observed that since the child's aloneness was reported from the 'beginning of life', then there must be a biological element at play. However, he also noted that overall family dynamics were often 'cold' and 'aloof'. This was later to form the basis of the now largely discredited 'refrigerator mother' theory of causation – in fact, as Feinstein observes (p.34), Kanner felt the need to formally 'acquit' parents of any blame relating to their children's autism in 1969, whilst addressing the first annual meeting of the National Society for Autistic Children in Washington DC.[111] Kanner did not become too involved in the treatment of children or adults with autism – his contribution was as an observer.

Hans Asperger (1906–1980)

Asperger, a paediatric physician, also from Austria, published the first formal definition of the syndrome that now bears his name in 1944.[112] He described four boys, in whom he described an 'autistic psychopathy'. The boys displayed a lack of empathy, poor social skills, an intense interest pattern, and clumsiness. The paper was published in German, at a time of intense suspicion of German medical practice. A complete English translation was not available until 1991, some 11 years after his death.[113] Lorna Wing (1981) first proposed the description of 'Asperger syndrome' having discovered his work over the previous decade.[114]

Bruno Bettelheim (1903–1990)

Although, in a sense, Bettelheim completes the triumvirate of Austrian pioneers within the field of autism, his story is by far the most controversial, and may explain some of the suspicion with which psychotherapeutic intervention (particularly psychoanalytic psychotherapy) for autism has been viewed. Much doubt has been cast on his qualifications and life story prior to arriving in America, having spent time in Nazi concentration camps.[115] In spite of a lack of evidence of either psychiatric or psychological training, he was appointed professor of psychology at the University of Chicago, and went on to become Director of the Sonia Shankman Orthogenic School, also in Chicago. It was here that he developed his theory of autism as being the result of 'refrigerator parenting', and that a cure could be reached only by separating the child from his or her parents. For Bettelheim, autism was nothing less than the child's defensive reaction against the wish of the parents that he or she no longer existed. His major work on this psychoanalytic approach, *The Empty Fortress* (1967)[116] was initially very well received, but there is now some doubt as to whether the children he was describing as having been 'cured' by his methods were actually autistic in the first place.[117]

Modern Ideas on Psychogenic Autism

First mooted by Leo Kanner, and popularised by Bruno Bettelheim, the term 'refrigerator mother' refers to the idea that autism is caused, according to Kanner (1943), by a lack of warmth and affect amongst the parents of children with autism,[118] and according to Bettelheim (1967, p.125), by a parent's desire that their child not exist (whether this desire was conscious or unconscious).[119] This led to the creation of theories about psychogenic autism (a condition arising from emotional or mental distress), with Bettelheim at the forefront. Such thinking has largely been discredited, not least because of the suspicions around falsification of some of Bettelheim's claims. However, there are still some modern-day proponents of the psychogenic ideas. As recently as February 2012, the clinical psychologist Tony Humphries published an article in Ireland[120] questioning the sole reliance on research into genetic and neurological causes for autism, calling instead for more understanding of some of the emotional back-stories of people on the autism spectrum. There was an implicit repetition of some of Bettelheim's ideas.

An interesting perspective on psychogenic autism is seen in the work of The Tavistock Autism Clinic, a service provided by the Tavistock and Portman NHS Foundation Trust, in London. Here, the view is taken that autism is a 'disorder of intersubjectivity' – a lack of the sense of other people. It is seen as an 'impairment of the normal *emotionally based curiosity about, and desire for, interpersonal relationships*'.[121] An organic cause is allowed, rather than the condition being the result of a defence against poor parenting. However, the presence of autism creates the circumstances for atypical development, and thereby the potential mismatch of expectations and understandings, resulting in emotional distress for both the child and those around them. This emotional distress will lead to defences being employed that can further shut the child off from the world around them. The psychoanalytic and psychodynamic approaches used at the clinic are designed to build relationships first between the child and the therapist (establishing rapport – see Chapter 1), and then between the child and the rest of his or her environment. The work is based on the idea of enabling a more robust development of personality – the essential creation of a 'self' with which to navigate 'other'.

The psychoanalytic approach employed at The Tavistock is based on intricate observation of a child, perhaps over several sessions. These observations then form the basis for interpretation – perhaps a client's repetitive behaviour is a defence against feeling separate from a caregiver, for example. For some reason, possibly organic, the child reacts badly to what is for typically developing children a necessary part of becoming a person. This 'personality' is thus interrupted, perhaps frozen, or delayed. The therapeutic work at the clinic in some ways seems very similar to Intensive Interaction, described in Chapter 6, at least in terms of the 'joining' of the spectrum client in his or her world. However, as Caldwell and Horwood (2008, p.37) point out, the proponents of

Intensive Interaction feel that the autistic withdrawal is more likely the result of sensory distortion or overwhelm.[122] Both psychoanalysts and Intensive Interactionists are aiming to provide 'safe spaces' – the former for personality to develop, the latter for sensory integration to take place. It may be the case that typical personality development can *only* take place once sensory integration has fully occurred, but that a different sensory processing style can enable the development of useful skills in art and design, for example, or understanding animal behaviour. Evidence for this can be found in the artwork of Donna Williams and Stephen Wiltshire, and the research of Temple Grandin into animal behavioural psychology (see the Bibliography).

Bernard Rimland (1928–2006)

Rimland was an experimental psychologist, whose interest in autism was sparked by the diagnosis of his son, born in 1956, with infantile autism. His research led to the publication of *Infantile Autism: The Syndrome and its Implications for a Neural Theory of Behavior* in 1964.[123] He founded the Autism Research Institute, and became a champion for those who felt that, rather than having an emotional cause, the key factor in autism was biochemical influences on neurodevelopment. This thinking became very popular amongst families who were tired of being accused of somehow causing their child's condition, and as a result the Autism Society of America was formed.

Rimland's career was not without controversy. He often expressed concern about the growing number of cases of autism, and attributed this to potential vaccine damage. He contributed a foreword to Miller's book on vaccines and autism in 2003.[124]

A major legacy of Rimland's work was an almost complete reversal of thinking about the causes and treatment of autism in the USA. Rimland himself observed in 1981 that *Infantile Autism* had successfully redirected psychological debate about autism from the preoccupation with psychodynamics to a 'more productive' interest in biology.[125] In his own words, he had exposed the 'psychogenic myths'. A potential problem resulting from this for some spectrum clients, whether children or adults, was the relative absence of therapeutic intervention aimed at emotional wellbeing – much intervention, if any, was for a couple of decades based around educational or behavioural systems, together with, for some, dietary intervention or supplements.

Nikolaas Tinbergen (1907–1988)

Tinbergen was a Dutch ethologist (studying the science of animal behaviour) and ornithologist. Amongst other things, he is credited with research (1951) into supernormal stimuli – artificial objects that produced a greater response from animals than their natural equivalent.[126] For example, he showed that birds would often prefer to sit on model eggs that were larger and more colourful than their own.

Tinbergen also developed a theory of autism (1986). Following his studies of shy children and animals, he noted the social stress prevalent in children on the spectrum, and proposed that interaction could be achieved using 'gentle' approaches.[127] Although Tinbergen acknowledged that there were theories of autism based around pathology and genetics, he maintained that much of the autistic 'presentation' was a reactive defence against environmental stress. He went on to advocate the now discredited and largely defunct 'holding therapy', in which children with autism in obvious distress were held on their mother's lap for as long as it took them to calm down (in some cases this was many hours). Whilst this practice would now be regarded as aversive, or even abusive, it is interesting to note the development of deep pressure techniques to aid relaxation (see Chapter 3).

Olga Bogdashina

Bogdashina has been Director of the first Day Centre for Autistic Children in Ukraine, and is President of the Autism Society of Ukraine. As the holder of a PhD in Linguistics, and the mother of a son with autism, she has developed a unique perspective on the 'language' of autism, combining this with a developing understanding of the sensory perceptual world of the spectrum. Her most succinct presentation of these ideas can be found in her 2010 publication, *Autism and the Edges of the Known World*.[128] Many practitioners will find her work illuminating and explanatory in terms of how people with autism might perceive the world around them.

Personal Accounts of Autism

It is interesting to note that the history of understanding and treating autism, certainly in psychotherapeutic terms, if not in education, for much of the last 70 years since Kanner's original paper[129] has been based on the observations of neurotypical people, sometimes struggling to make sense of it all. Whilst some of these observations have been erudite and informative, there have been some extraordinary assumptions and conclusions, not least of which was Bettelheim's assertion that inadequate parenting was somehow a direct cause of autism.[130] These assumptions may have set back the cause of supporting emotional wellbeing in autism by several decades. However, particularly over the last 15 years, several people with autism have 'found their voices' and are providing fascinating glimpses of many of the individual facets of life on the spectrum. These personal accounts have informed us, amongst other things, of the rich inner life that it is possible to experience on the spectrum, the emotional distress that is caused by trying to navigate a social world not designed for an 'autistic' mind and the alternative sensory perspectives that are prevalent. It is not possible to do justice to all of the spectrum contributors to our knowledge but, with apologies to those not mentioned, I have provided a list of resources in the 'Further Reading' section at the end of this book. This should, at least, be a starting point for those wishing to acquaint themselves further with what it is like to inhabit the autism spectrum.

Autism Rights Movements

As well as providing personal accounts of living with autism, many people on the spectrum are finding opportunities for collective advocacy through organisations run by people with autism for people with autism. Examples include Autism Network International,[131] and Autistic Rights Movement UK.[132] The organisations tend to be anti-'cure', and promote greater acceptance of 'autistic' behaviours alongside treatment interventions that focus on teaching coping skills and enhancing social networks. Many of the interventions described above have these aims in mind. The organisations also provide scope for a political voice, and actively seek ways of representing their communities' views to local and national governments.

Endnotes

1   Moat (2011).

2   Goodyear (2008).

3   Kanner (1969).

4   Shepherd (2011).

5   Goleman (1996).

6   Fleming (2012).

7   Grandin (1996).

8   Bogdashina (2003).

9   Williams (1998).

10 West (2007).

11 Gaus (2007).

12 Jacobsen (2003).

13 Paxton and Estay (2007).

14 Richards and Borglin (2011).

15 Leichsenring (2001).

16 Attwood (1998).

17 Paxton and Estay (2007).

18 Goodyear (2008).

19 Mitchell (2008).

20 Caldwell (2007).

21 Hewett, Firth, Barber and Harrison (2011).

22 Moat (2008).

23   Hollins (2000).

24   Howlin (2004).

25   Blackman (2003).

26   Jacobson (1938).

27   Craske and Barlow (2006).

28   Bogdashina (2003).

29   Grandin (1992).

30   Pyles (2002).

31   Lawson (2012).

32   James and Gilliland (2011).

33   Jordan and Jones (1999).

34   Anderson (2012).

35   Grandin (2011).

36   Ibid.

37   Ramsay and Compton (2011).

38   Fernandes (2009).

39   Buglione (2011).

40   Jung, Sepers, Henstridge, Lassalle *et al.* (2012).

41   Shapiro and Sprague (2009).

42   Sams, Fortney and Willenbring (2006).

43   Pavlides (2008).

44   Moat (2008).

45   White (2006).

46   Moat (2008).

47   Garcia Winner (2002).

48   Patrick (2008).

49   Gray (1994).

50   Grandin and Barron (2005).

51   Aston (2003).

52   Paxton and Estay (2007).

53   Vroom (1964).

54   Gaus (2007).

55   Caldwell (2007).

56   Hewett *et al.* (2011).

57   Kaufman (1995).

58   Lovaas (1987).

59   Jenkins, Schuchard and Thompson (2012).

60   Caldwell and Horwood (2008) .

61   Wilbarger and Wilbarger (1991).

62   Williams (1996).

63   Lawson (1998).

64   Bogdashina (2004).

65   Bogdashina (2003).

66   Usher (2012).

67   Beyer and Gammeltoft (2000).

68   Herrera, Alcantud, Jordan, Blanquer, Labajo and De Pablo (2008).

69   Vickers and Zollman (1999).

70   Heap, Alden, Brown, Naish *et al.* (2001).

71   Yapko (2006).

72   Bogdashina (2010).

73   Williams (1998).

74   Yapko (2006).

75   Heather (2011).

76   Grandin (1996).

77   Coué (2006).

78   Mesibov, Shea and Schopler (2005).

79   Leuner (1969).

80   National Institute for Health and Clinical Excellence (NICE) (2012).

81   Paxton and Estay (2007).

82   Attwood (2004).

83   Ibid.

84   Goodyear (2008).

85   Greene and Ablon (2006).

86   Sylvers, Lilienfeld and LaPrairie (2011).

87   Dunn Buron and Curtis (2003).

88   Paxton and Estay (2007).

89   Cresswell and Willetts (2007).

90   Heather (2011).

91   Attwood (1998).

92   NICE (2012).

93   Paxton and Estay (2007).

94   Forrester-Jones and Broadhurst (2008).

95   Allison (2001).

96   Worden (1991).

97   Gates (2007).

98   O'Brien, Pearpoint and Kahn (2010).

99   Hollins (2000).

100 Craig (2011).

101 Fenstein (2012).

102 Lewis (2007).

103 Carroll (2012a).

104 Shapiro and Forrest (1997).

105 Carroll (2012b).

106 Shapiro and Forrest (1997).

107 Morris-Smith (2007).

108 Mevissen, Lievegoed and de Jongh (2011).

109 Feinstein (2010).

110 Kanner (1943).

111 Feinstein (2010).

112 Asperger (1944).

113 Frith (ed.) (1991).

114 Wing (1981).

115 Pollak (1998).

116 Bettelheim (1967).

117 Finn (1997).

118 Kanner (1943).

119 Bettelheim (1967).

120 *Irish Examiner, The* (2012).

121 Alvarez and Reid (eds) (1999).

122 Caldwell and Horwood (2008).

123 Rimland (1964).

124 Miller (2003).

125 Rimland (1981).

126 Tinbergen (1951).

127 Tinbergen and Tinbergen (1986).

128 Bogdashina (2010).

129 Kanner (1943).

130 Bettelheim (1967).

131 See www.autreat.com, accessed on 12 December 2012.

132 See www.autisticrightsmovementuk.org, accessed on 12 December 2012.

Bibliography

Allison, H.G. (2001) *Support for the Bereaved and Dying in Services for Adults with Autistic Spectrum Disorders.* London: The National Autistic Society.

Alvarez, A. and Reid, S. (eds) (1999) *Autism and Personality: Findings from the Tavistock Autism Workshop.* London: Routledge.

Anderson, E.G. (2012) *What is Rebound Therapy.* Available at www.reboundtherapy.org/?p=whatis, accessed on 19 December 2012.

Asperger, H. (1944) 'Die "Autistischen Psychopathen" im Kindesalter.' *Archiv für psychiatrie und nervenkrankheiten 117,* 76–136.

Aston, M. (2003) 'Asperger Syndrome in the counselling room.' *Counselling and Psychotherapy Journal 14,* 5, 10–14.

Attwood, T. (1998) *Asperger's Syndrome: A Guide for Parents and Professionals.* London: Jessica Kingsley Publishers.

Attwood, T. (2004) *Exploring Feelings: Cognitive Behavior Therapy to Manage Anger.* Arlington, TX: Future Horizons.

Bettelheim, B. (1967) *The Empty Fortress: Infantile Autism and the Birth of the Self.* New York: Free Press.

Beyer, J. and Gammeltoft, L. (2000) *Autism and Play.* London: Jessica Kingsley Publishers.

Blackman, N. (2003) *Loss and Learning Disability.* London: Worth Publishing Ltd.

Bogdashina, O. (2003) *Sensory Perceptual Issues in Autism and Asperger Syndrome: Different Sensory Experiences – Different Perceptual Worlds.* London: Jessica Kingsley Publishers.

Bogdashina, O. (2004) *Communication Issues in Autism and Asperger Syndrome.* London: Jessica Kingsley Publishers.

Bogdashina, O. (2010) *Autism and the Edges of the Known World.* London: Jessica Kingsley Publishers.

Buglione, N. (2011) *Marijuana Madness*. Autism Support Network. Available at www.autismsupportnetwork.com/news/autism-treatment-marijuana-madness-8763721, accessed on 20 November 2012.

Caldwell, P. (2007) *From Isolation to Intimacy: Making Friends Without Words*. London: Jessica Kingsley Publishers.

Caldwell, P. and Horwood, J. (2008) *Using Intensive Interaction and Sensory Integration*. London: Jessica Kingsley Publishers.

Carroll, R.T. (2012a) *Emotional Freedom Techniques. Davis, CA: The Skeptic's Dictionary*. Available at www.skepdic.com/eft.html, accessed on 27 October 2012.

Carroll, R.T. (2012b) *Eye Movement Desensitization and Reprocessing (EMDR)*. Davis, CA: The Skeptic's Dictionary. Available at www.skepdic.com/emdr.html, accessed on 27 October 2012.

Coué, É. (2006) *Self Mastery Through Conscious Autosuggestion*. Stilwell, KS: digireads.com (original work published 1922).

Craig, G. (2011) *The EFT Manual (2nd Edition)*. Fulton, CA: Energy Psychology Press.

Craske, M. and Barlow, D. (2006) *Mastery of Your Anxiety and Worry*. New York: Oxford University Press.

Cresswell, C. and Willetts, L. (2007) *Overcoming Your Child's Fears and Worries: A Self-Help Guide Using Cognitive Behavioural Techniques*. London: Constable and Robinson.

Dunn Buron, K. and Curtis, M. (2003) *The Incredible 5-Point Scale*. Shawnee Mission, KS: Autism Asperger Publishing Company.

Feinstein, A. (2010) *A History of Autism: Conversations with the Pioneers*. Chichester: Wiley-Blackwell.

Fenstein, D. (2012) 'Acupoint stimulation in treating psychological disorders: evidence of efficacy.' *American Psychological Association Review of General Psychology 16*, 4, 364–380.

Fernandes, G.K. (2009) *Can Marijuana Help Kids with Autism?* Momlogic. Available at www.momlogic.com/2009/11/can_marijuana_help_kids_with_autism.php, accessed on 20 November 2012.

Fleming, N. (2012) *VARK: A Guide to Learning Styles*. Available at www.vark-learn.com, accessed on 29 October 2012.

Finn, M. (1997) 'In the case of Bruno Bettelheim.' *First Things 74*, 44–48.

Forrester-Jones, R. and Broadhurst, S. (2008) *Autism and Loss*. London: Jessica Kingsley Publishers.

Frederick, C. and McNeal, S.A. (1998) *Inner Strengths: Contemporary Psychotherapy and Hypnosis for Ego-Strengthening*. New Jersey: Lawrence Earlbaum Associates.

Frith, U. (ed.) (1991) *Autism and Asperger Syndrome*. Cambridge: Cambridge University Press.

Garcia Winner, M. (2002) 'Assessment of social skills for students with Asperger Syndrome and high-functioning autism.' *Assessment for Effective Intervention 27*, 1–2, 73–80.

Gates, B. (2007) *Learning Disabilities: Towards Inclusion*. London: Churchill Livingstone.

Gaus, V. (2007) *Cognitive Behavioral Therapy for Adult Asperger Syndrome*. New York: Guilford Press.

Goleman, D. (1996) *Emotional Intelligence*. London: Bloomsbury.

Goodyear, B. (2008) *Coaching People with Asperger Syndrome*. London: Karnac.

Grandin, T. (1992) 'Calming effects of deep touch pressure in patients with autistic disorder, college students and animals.' *Journal of Child and Adult Psychopharmacology 2*, 1, 63–72.

Grandin, T. (1996) *Thinking in Pictures and Other Reports from My Life with Autism*. New York: Vintage.

Grandin, T. (2011) *The Way I See It: A Personal Look at Autism and Asperger's*. Arlington, TX: Future Horizons.

Grandin, T. and Barron, S. (2005) *Unwritten Rules of Social Relationships: Decoding Social Mysteries through the Unique Perspectives of Autism*. Arlington, TX: Future Horizons.

Grandin, T. and Johnson, C. (2006) *Animals in Translation: The Woman Who Thinks Like a Cow*. London: Bloomsbury.

Gray, C. (1994) *The Social Story Book*. Arlington, TX: Future Horizons.

Greene, R. and Ablon, S. (2006) *Treating Explosive Kids: The Collaborative Problem Solving Approach*. New York: Guilford Press.

Heap, M., Alden, P., Brown, R., Naish, P. *et al.* (2001) *The Nature of Hypnosis*. Leicester: British Psychological Society.

Heather, D. (2011) *Asperger Personalities, Anxiety and Hypnosis*. Available at lulu.com, accessed March 28, 2013.

Herrera, G., Alcantud, F., Jordan, R., Blanquer, A., Labajo, G. and De Pablo, C. (2008) 'Development of symbolic play through the use of virtual reality tools in children with autistic spectrum disorders.' *Autism 12*, 2, 143–157.

Hewett, D., Firth, G., Barber, M. and Harrison, T. (2011) *The Intensive Interaction Handbook*. London: Sage Publications.

Hollins, S. (2000) 'Developmental psychiatry – insights from learning disability.' *British Journal of Psychiatry 177*, 201–206.

Howlin, P. (2004) *Autism and Asperger Syndrome: Preparing for Adulthood*. London: Routledge.

Irish Examiner, The (2012) 'Core Connections', 3 February, FeelGood Supplement.

Jacobsen, P. (2003) *Asperger Syndrome and Psychotherapy: Understanding Asperger Perspectives.* London: Jessica Kingsley Publishers.

Jacobson, E. (1938) *Progressive Relaxation.* Chicago, IL: University of Chicago Press.

James, R.K. and Gilliland, B.E. (2011) *Crisis Intervention Strategies.* Mason, OH: Cengage Learning Inc.

Jenkins, T., Schuchard, J. and Thompson, C.K. (2012) *Training Parents to Promote Communication and Social Behavior in Children with Autism: The Son-Rise Program. Autism Treatment Center.* Available at www.autismtreatmentcenter. org, accessed on 1 December 2012.

Jordan, R. and Jones, G. (1999) *Meeting the Needs of Children with Autistic Spectrum Disorders.* London: David Fulton Publishers.

Jung, K.M., Sepers, M., Henstridge, C.M., Lassalle, O. *et al.* (2012) 'Uncoupling of the endocannabinoid signalling complex in a mouse model of fragile X syndrome.' *Nature Communication 3,* 1080.

Kanner, L. (1943) 'Autistic disturbances of affective contact.' *Nervous Child,* 2, 217–250.

Kanner, L. (1969) Interview published in the *Baltimore Sun,* 13 July. Cited in A. Feinstein (2010) *A History of Autism: Conversations with the Pioneers.* Chichester: Wiley-Blackwell.

Kaufman, B.N. (1995) *Son Rise: The Miracle Continues.* Tiburon, CA: H.J. Kramer.

Lawson, W. (1998) *My Life with Asperger Syndrome.* Available at www.mugsy. org/wendy/qanda, accessed on 24 November 2012.

Lawson, W. (2012) *Testimonials Page.* SQUEASE. Available at www.squeasewear. com/en/testimonials, accessed on 19 November 2012.

Leichsenring, F. (2001) 'Comparative effects of short-term psychodynamic psychotherapy and cognitive behavioural therapy in depression: a meta-analytic approach.' *Clinical Psychology Review 21,* 3, 401–419.

Leuner, H. (1969) 'Guided Affective Imagery (GAI): a method of intensive psychotherapy.' *American Journal of Psychotherapy 23,* 1, 4–22.

Lewis, S. (2007) *Using EFT on Autism with Dramatic Results.* Toronto: Artemis Psychotherapy. Available at www.artemistherapy.com/page7.html, accessed on 22 October 2012.

Lovaas, O.I. (1987) 'Behavioral treatment and normal intellectual and educational functioning in autistic children.' *Journal of Consulting and Clinical Psychology 55,* 1, 3–9.

Mesibov, G., Shea, V. and Schopler, E. (2005) *The TEACCH Approach to Autism Spectrum Disorders.* New York: Plenum Publishing Co.

Mevissen, L., Lievegoed, R. and de Jongh, A. (2011) 'EMDR treatment in people with mild ID and PTSD: 4 cases.' *The Psychiatric Quarterly 83*, 1, 43–57.

Miller, N.Z. (2003) *Vaccines, Autism and Childhood Disorders: Crucial Data That Could Save Your Child's Life*. Sante Fe, NM: New Atlantean Press.

Mitchell, C. (2008) *Asperger's Syndrome and Mindfulness: Taking Refuge in The Buddha*. London: Jessica Kingsley Publishers.

Moat, D. (2008) *Asperger Syndrome: Social Intervention Skills Training*. Cambridge: Autism Quality SEARCH.

Moat, D. (2011) *Hearts of Glass: Integrative Psychotherapeutic Approaches to Autism. Conference abstract: Newer Interventions in the Case of Autism and Other Degenerative Disorders*, Tervisekool, Tartu, Estonia.

Morris-Smith, J. (2007) 'EMDR and children: Europe leads the way.' *Therapy Today 18*, 3, 9–12.

National Institute for Health and Clinical Excellence (NICE) (2012) *Autism: Recognition, Referral, Diagnosis and Management of Adults on the Autism Spectrum*. London: NICE. Available at www.publications.nice.org.uk/autism-recognition-referral-diagnosis-and-management-of-adults-on-the-autism-spectrum-cg142, accessed on 5 March 2013.

O'Brien, J., Pearpoint, J. and Kahn, L. (2010) *The PATHS and MAPS Handbook: Person-Centred Ways to Build Community*. Toronto: Inclusion Press.

Patrick, N.J. (2008) *Social Skills for Teenagers and Adults with Asperger Syndrome*. Philadelphia, PA: Jessica Kingsley Publishers.

Pavlides, M. (2008) *Animal-Assisted Interventions for Individuals with Autism*. London: Jessica Kingsley Publishers.

Paxton, K. and Estay, I. (2007) *Counselling People on the Autism Spectrum: A Practical Manual*. Philadelphia, PA: Jessica Kingsley Publishers.

Pollak, R. (1998) *The Creation of Dr B: A Biography of Bruno Bettelheim*. New York: Touchstone.

Pyles, L. (2002) *Hitchhiking through Asperger Syndrome*. London: Jessica Kingsley Publishers.

Ramsay, C.E. and Compton, M.T. (2011) 'The Interface of Cannabis Misuse and Schizophrenia Spectrum Disorders.' In M. Ritsner (ed.) *Handbook of Schizophrenia Spectrum Disorders, Volume 111: Therapeutic Approaches, Comorbidity and Outcomes*. Dordrecht, NL: Springer.

Richards, D.A. and Borglin, G. (2011) 'Implementation of psychological therapies for anxiety and depression in routine practice: two year prospective cohort study.' *Journal of Affective Disorders 133*, 1–2, 51–60.

Rimland, R. (1964) *Infantile Autism: The Syndrome and its Implications for a Neural Theory of Behavior*. New York: Appleton Century Crofts.

Rimland, R. (1981) *This Week's Classic Citation.* The Garfield Library. Available at www.garfield.library.upenn.edu/classics1981/A1981LQ21000001.pdf, accessed on 13 December 2012.

Sams, M.J., Fortney, E.V. and Willenbring, S. (2006) 'Occupational therapy incorporating animals for children with autism: a pilot investigation.' *American Occupational Therapy Association 60*, 3, 268–274.

Shapiro, F. and Forrest, M.S. (1997) *EMDR: The Breakthrough 'Eye Movement' Therapy for Overcoming Anxiety, Stress and Trauma.* New York: Basic Books.

Shapiro, L. and Sprague, R. (2009) *The Relaxation and Stress Reduction Workbook for Kids.* Oakland, CA: New Harbinger Productions.

Shepherd, N. (2011) 'It's All in Your Head: The Dangers of Misdiagnosis.' In L. Beardon and D. Worton (eds) *Aspies on Mental Health: Speaking for Ourselves.* London: Jessica Kingsley Publishers.

Sylvers, P., Lilienfeld, S.O. and LaPrairie, J.L. (2011) 'Difficulties between trait and fear anxiety: implications for psychopathology.' *Clinical Psychology Review 31*, 1, 122–137.

Tinbergen, N. (1951) *The Study of Instinct.* Oxford: Clarendon Press.

Tinbergen, N. and Tinbergen, E.A. (1986) *Autistic Children: New Hope for a Cure.* London: Routledge.

Usher, W. (2012) 'Autism and play: taking a child centred approach.' *Better Breaks: The Online Journal for the Short Break Sector.* Short Breaks Network. Available at www.shortbreaksnetwork.org.uk/policyandpractice/better breaks/previousissues, accessed on 25 November 2012.

Vickers, A. and Zollman, C. (1999) 'Hypnosis and relaxation therapies.' *British Medical Journal 319*, 7221, 1346–1349.

Vroom, V. (1964) *Work and Motivation.* New York: John Wiley and Sons.

West, O. (2007) *In Search of Words: Footnotes Visual Thinking Techniques.* Penzance: O. West.

White, C. (2006) *The Social Play Record.* London: Jessica Kingsley Publishers.

Wilbarger, P. and Wilbarger, J. (1991) *Sensory Defensiveness in Children Ages 2–12: An Intervention Guide for Parents and Other Caretakers.* Santa Barbara, CA: Avanti Educational Programs.

Williams, D. (1996) *Autism – An Inside-Out Approach.* London: Jessica Kingsley Publishers.

Williams, D. (1998) *Autism and Sensing: The Unlost Instinct.* London: Jessica Kingsley Publishers.

Williams, D. (2011) *Donna Williams: The Artist.* Australia: Donna Williams. Available at www.donnawilliams.net/artist.0.html, accessed on 5 March 2013.

Wiltshire, S. (2013) *Stephen Wiltshire.* London: Stephen Wiltshire. Available at www.stephenwiltshire.co.uk, accessed on 5 March 2013.

Wing, L. (1981) 'Asperger syndrome: a clinical account.' *Psychological Medicine 11*, 1, 115–129.

Worden, J.W. (1991) *Grief Counselling and Grief Therapy: A Handbook for the Mental Health Practitioner.* London: Routledge.

Yapko, D. (2006) 'The Utilization Approach to Treating Depression in Individuals with Autistic Spectrum Disorders.' In M. Yapko (ed.) *Hypnosis and Treating Depression.* London: Routledge.

Yapko, M. (ed.) (2006) *Hypnosis and Treating Depression.* London: Routledge.

Further Reading
Personal Accounts of Life on the Spectrum

Beardon, L. and Worton, D. (2011) *Aspies on Mental Health: Speaking for Ourselves*. London: Jessica Kingsley Publishers.

Grandin, T. (1996) *Thinking in Pictures and Other Reports from My Life with Autism*. New York: Vintage.

Holliday Willey, L. (1999) *Pretending to be Normal: Living with Asperger's Syndrome*. London: Jessica Kingsley Publishers.

Jackson, L. (2002) *Freaks, Geeks and Asperger Syndrome*. London: Jessica Kingsley Publishers.

Jackson, N. (2002) *Standing Up, Falling Down*. Bristol: Lucky Duck Publishing.

Lawson, W. (2000) *Life Behind Glass: A Personal Account of Autism Spectrum Disorder*. London: Jessica Kingsley Publishers.

Williams, D. (1998a) *Nobody Nowhere*. London: Jessica Kingsley Publishers.

Williams, D. (1998b) *Somebody Somewhere*. London: Jessica Kingsley Publishers.

Williams, D. (2008) *Exposure Anxiety – The Invisible Cage: An Exploration of Self-Protection Responses in the Autism Spectrum and Beyond*. London: Jessica Kingsley Publishers.

Websites

Autism Resources. Available at www.autism-resources.com/links/accounts.html

The National Autistic Society. Available at www.autism.org.uk/living-with-autism/real-life-stories/real-life-stories-from-people-with-autism.aspx

Personal Stories about Autism Spectrum Disorders. Available at www.autism-help.org/personal-stories-autism-aspergers.htm

Research Autism. Available at www.researchautism.net/pages/autism_autistic_asperger_spectrum/personal_accounts_autism/

Subject Index

Author Index